Training Library Patrons the ADDIE Way

CHANDOS
INFORMATION PROFESSIONAL SERIES

Series Editor: Ruth Rikowski
(email: Rikowskigr@aol.com)

Chandos' new series of books are aimed at the busy information professional. They have been specially commissioned to provide the reader with an authoritative view of current thinking. They are designed to provide easy-to-read and (most importantly) practical coverage of topics that are of interest to librarians and other information professionals. If you would like a full listing of current and forthcoming titles, please visit our web site **www.chandospublishing.com** or contact Hannah Grace-Williams on email info@chandospublishing.com or telephone number +44 (0) 1865 884447.

New authors: we are always pleased to receive ideas for new titles; if you would like to write a book for Chandos, please contact Dr Glyn Jones on email gjones@chandospublishing.com or telephone number +44 (0) 1865 884447.

Bulk orders: some organisations buy a number of copies of our books. If you are interested in doing this, we would be pleased to discuss a discount. Please contact Hannah Grace-Williams on email info@chandospublishing.com or telephone number +44 (0) 1865 884447.

Training Library Patrons
the ADDIE Way

D. R. WEGENER

Chandos Publishing
Oxford · England

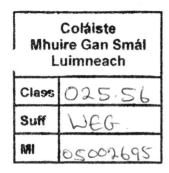
Chandos Publishing (Oxford) Limited
Chandos House
5 & 6 Steadys Lane
Stanton Harcourt
Oxford OX29 5RL
UK
Tel: +44 (0) 1865 884447 Fax: +44 (0) 1865 884448
Email: info@chandospublishing.com
www.chandospublishing.com

First published in Great Britain in 2006

ISBN:
1 84334 157 3 (paperback)
1 84334 168 9 (hardback)
978 1 84334 157 4 (paperback)
978 1 84334 168 0 (hardback)

Typeset by Domex e-Data Pvt. Ltd.
Printed in the UK and USA.

Contents

List of figures

Figures

Acknowledgements

My heartfelt thanks go to those who so willingly gave me permission to use their work, or the work of their institutions. They include Yannis Grammatis, David Burns from Magna Publications; and all those people from:

- California Polytechnic State University Library;
- Cornell University Library;
- James Cook University;
- Queensland University of Technology Library;
- University of Limerick Library;
- University of South Australia Library;
- University of Technology in Sydney; and
- University of Wyoming Libraries.

I would also like to express my appreciation to those people who responded so readily to my requests for quotes and stories. My grateful thanks go to Eng Mui Hong, Sandra J. Kemp, Ling Ai Li Alice, Madi McAllister, Rajendra Munoo, Susie Spies and Triffie Vorster.

And last but not least, my thanks go to Dr Glyn Jones for asking, to the Temasek Polytechnic in Singapore for providing the opportunity, and to Jethro John for his patience.

Preface

When I first started training, I needed to find a book that would help me with everything, in other words, with preparing, developing, presenting and delivering an entire training session. I needed to know how to do all of this in a library situation and, above all, I needed to know if anyone else had actually managed to fog up their reading glasses by having all the blood rush to their face in an embarrassing moment. Well, I did manage to find all this information, except for the part about the reading glasses, but I couldn't find it all logically organised into a single book. I also found that a lot of the really good stuff on training is not written by librarians, but by training professionals and presenters who take a slightly different stance from the one that we need to take for library patrons.

The purpose of this book, therefore, is to bring as much of this information as possible together under one title for anyone who has to train in libraries, and for the new and nervous trainer in particular. The basic premise is that as long as you are prepared and have your back-up plans in place, the whole process of training becomes much less stressful and, consequently, much more successful. Organised according to the ADDIE model of instructional design, the chapters of this book follow the ADDIE steps of:

- analysis;
- design;

- development;
- implementation; and
- evaluation.

With a brief introduction and conclusion, hints and tips and suggestions are given throughout, as well as a few educational theories to raise your awareness of trainee learning styles and motivation and to help with the development of your objectives. It is also strongly suggested that you look at what other librarians have been doing, hence a few of my favourite online information literacy programmes are discussed. In the appendices you will find a learning style survey, examples of lesson plans, and a number of annotated articles on the instructional experiences of librarians around the world. As for the bit about fogging up one's reading glasses, well, I haven't found anything yet, but I can tell you that until I learned to relax, I stopped wearing my glasses in training sessions.

About the author

Debby R. Wegener is a reference librarian at the Temasek Polytechnic Library in Singapore. She was born and bred in Zimbabwe and started her career in the library world as a part-time circulation assistant at the Rhodes University Library in Grahamstown, South Africa. After completing a Master of Applied Science (Information Studies) from Charles Sturt University in Australia, she worked for a while as a trainer for a library systems vendor. Debby is also editor of the Temasek Polytechnic Library's quarterly newsletter, webmaster of the library's website, and coordinator of the library's information literacy programme.

The author may be contacted via the publisher.

Introduction

She could almost feel the control slipping away from her as she listened to the question with a dawning sense of panic. This training session wasn't supposed to deal with cataloguing rules! It was about how to use the new library system's cataloguing module. The schedule was tight enough already without having to try and deal with questions on obscure topics like initial title elements and corporate headings. They hadn't got halfway through this module yet, and tomorrow they had to start on the serials section. How on earth was she going to finish on time if they didn't stick to the topic and stop asking useless questions?

Anyone who has ever had to design a training programme will know that it can be quite a daunting task. Where do you begin, for example, if you only have one week to train 1,000 new college students to use a library system when there are only 25 computers in your training room? Would an existing programme work, or does a totally new one have to be devised? Can the trainees share the computers, or must they each have their own workstation? Do they really need a hands-on, face-to-face kind of situation, or would a lecture-style delivery work? Perhaps an online programme would be an even better option?

Whichever approach you decide to take, it is always useful to have a systematic way of making sure that nothing is overlooked because, as I have found, it can be very easy to get yourself into an awkward situation. Take, for example, the frantic thoughts in the previous excerpt from a trainer who found herself in just such a situation.

The trainer in this case had assumed that the title of the session was self-explanatory and, in an effort to save time, had not provided any training objectives. It doesn't take much of an imagination to predict the direction that the rest of her training session would have taken. The mad dash through the remainder of the module in an effort to keep to the schedule; the growing irritation of the trainees as they found themselves wondering just what kind of trainer they were paying for – she seemed to be avoiding all of their most burning questions! All in all, this scenario points to a most unsatisfactory training session for the trainer and the trainees. If the trainer had just followed a few simple guidelines, however, she could have avoided this situation altogether. And this is where instructional systems design or instructional systems development (ISD) can come in extremely handy.

Instructional systems design

Very simply, ISD is an approach to training that allows you to decide:

- who;
- what;
- when;
- where;

- why;

- how.

Organised into logical steps, this system allows you to deal with all the aspects that are involved in the creation of a training programme. This approach will also work regardless of whether the programme is going to be delivered face-to-face in a workshop, or online via distance education. ISD has a number of different theories and approaches that can be used by trainers, but I have found the ADDIE model to be particularly effective in that it takes a learner-centred approach.

A learner-centred approach, to my mind, is the best one, as it focuses on the needs of the trainee, as opposed to the needs of the trainer. As Barkley and Bianco (2001) point out, the most basic mistake made is that, instead of giving the trainees what they want, the trainers teach what they think is best – a sort of 'I know what's good for you' approach. In the library world, this is perfectly understandable, in that we usually need to train patrons to use our library systems – often we don't have much of a choice. Our biggest problems arise, however, when we start asking if our patrons are motivated and eager to learn this type of thing in an organised training session.

In my experience, our patrons are hardly ever excited about having to attend a library workshop and, without the necessary motivation, there isn't much incentive to learn. If trainees cannot find relevance or meaning in a topic, they are hardly likely to be happy about it, and the possibility of any actual learning taking place starts looking very remote. To make it possible for learning to actually happen, we need to encourage the trainees to personally feel that they want to learn, and following the ADDIE model can help us to do just this.

The ADDIE model basically takes you through the steps of analysis, design, development, implementation and evaluation when designing a training programme. As far as we know, the ADDIE model first surfaced in the 1970s when an instructional systems development model was created, which included the steps of analysing, designing, developing, implementing and controlling (Molenda, 2003). Interesting to note is that, just like with the World Wide Web, the US Department of Defense was involved here. Over the years this model seems to have been reworked and revised to the point where in the ADDIE model of today, the control phase has become the evaluation phase.

Different variations

ISD has been described as a model that takes a systematic approach to the design of training programmes, although there are some who disagree with the use of the word 'systematic'. Visscher-Voerman and Gustafson (2004) conducted a study where they found that instructional designers in the real world don't actually follow the rigidly organised, step-by-step approach suggested by the ADDIE acronym. They argue that instead, the designers select the parts of each stage that they feel are important, and they use these parts whenever and wherever they feel it necessary.

Molenda (2003) even goes so far as to lament the loss of what he calls 'academic rigor' as we all seem to interpret ADDIE according to our own needs. However, I would tend to agree with the findings of Visscher-Voerman and Gustafson. For example, if you already have a programme that just needs to be updated, you could start with evaluation and not analysis, and ignore some of the points from the other stages. After all, the ADDIE model is a set of guidelines, not a list of rules that have been cast in stone.

Various researchers have portrayed the different stages of the ADDIE model in different ways, so I have provided different examples to give you an idea of the varying points of view (see Figures 1.1 to 1.4). Each version, however, makes use of the same basic five stages:

- *Analysis* – thinking about the trainees.
- *Design* – considering the objectives.
- *Development* – creating the course.
- *Implementation* – delivering the goods.
- *Evaluation* – deciding if it really worked.

In Figure 1.1, Molenda (2003) sees ADDIE as process that begins with analysis and moves on through to evaluation. At each stage, however, the designer may need to return to the previous stage or repeat another stage before moving on, while evaluation can take place at any time.

Figure 1.1   Molenda's version of the ADDIE model

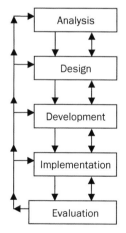

Figure 1.2 Brandt's version of the ADDIE model

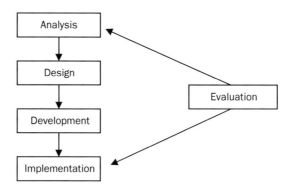

Brandt's (2002) view in Figure 1.2 appears very similar to that of Molenda's. The Instructional Technology Services department from the Texas A&M University (2001), on the other hand, portrays ADDIE as a loop (see Figure 1.3) where each stage is regularly repeated with a view to further improvements.

Similarly, in Figure 1.4, Clark (1995) shows that training is not a rigid type of model where you always start with analysis and end with evaluation. He prefers to see the process as much more dynamic. He does emphasise, however, that evaluation and feedback are constantly required, no matter which stage you are in.

Figure 1.3 The Texas A&M University version of the ADDIE model

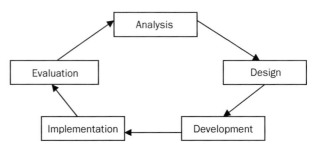

Figure 1.4   Clark's version of the ADDIE model

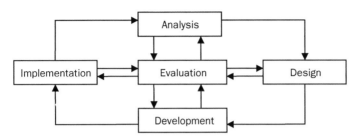

Sometimes the tasks contained in each stage will also vary slightly according to the researcher. Watson (2002), for example, places the formulation of objectives in the analysis phase, while I feel it is more logical to look at your objectives in the design stage. I wouldn't imagine it makes all that much difference in the long run, however, as long as you cater for the points in all the stages whenever necessary.

Flexibility

When it comes to the diagrams, the one that seems to make the most sense to me is the one provided by Clark (1995) in Figure 1.4. This is because the ADDIE model is actually flexible enough to allow you to start anywhere, and to jump backwards and forwards as and when you feel it is necessary. It can be useful to evaluate your efforts after every stage, especially if you are new to ISD, and feedback from the learners or colleagues during implementation in particular, can be extremely valuable. You may even prefer to begin with the evaluation of another programme, using those findings to design improvements in your new programme. It doesn't matter how you prepare for your training session, as long as you prepare.

Preparation, preparation, preparation

> Before anything else, preparation is the key to success.
> (Alexander Graham Bell)

For some people, having to conduct training is an ordeal they would prefer not to have to endure. Being in the spotlight under the watchful gaze of so many eyes can be too intimidating, especially for those of us who consider ourselves to be introverts. Careful preparation, however, can make the whole training experience far more successful and far less harrowing. If I had been better prepared, for example, I could have avoided the situation described in the excerpt at the beginning of this chapter!

As research has shown that training programmes are more likely to be successful if they follow a well-prepared lesson plan, the ADDIE model can make the preparation of such a plan that much easier. This book will take an informal, in-depth look at each stage of the ADDIE model, including hints and tips and quotes from experienced trainers at each of the stages. Written with the novice trainer in mind, the aim is to show that while training can be daunting and difficult, it can also be rewarding and extremely satisfying. You simply need to have the right attitude, some expert advice and, of course, a plan!

2

Analysis: think about the trainees

- Who are your *trainees*?
- What do they *need to learn*?
- What are your *performance measures*?
- What are your *delivery options*?
- Are there any *constraints*?
- Is there a *budget*?
- What is your *time limit*?

In the analysis stage of the ADDIE model, your primary focus should be on your target audience, that is, your trainees. As the first question asked by most trainees is usually 'What's in it for me?', you need to know as much as possible about this group of people in order to be able to answer this question to their satisfaction. One of the main priorities in training is, of course, the satisfaction of the trainees. As a colleague of mine put it, in relation to training adults:

> When I'm planning training, one of the most important areas for me is making sure I know the goals of the participants who will attend the training. Different groups have different approaches to learning in a

workshop setting. Sometimes the training can be just an escape from a busy office or gives the participant time to think about something different. Often participants attend to get tips and techniques about that topic, but sometimes the main objective is to have a solution to solving a critical problem in the workplace. For me as a trainer, I think the most important ingredient for successful training is 'knowing' the participants. (Sandra J. Kemp – lecturer, Singapore)

No two exactly the same

One of the most interesting aspects of training is that each group of people being trained is different. You may have to deliver the same content to 17 groups of students from the same class, for example, but no two training sessions will be exactly the same. One group of trainees may solve the problems that you set very quickly, while another group will spend more time asking you questions. In spite of the fact that you are saying essentially the same thing in every session, you may find that your delivery usually needs to be altered slightly each time to cater for each particular group's needs.

Then again, the fact that no two groups are the same is also one of the most challenging aspects of training. You may find that in your first session, the trainees find your favourite anecdote exquisitely humorous, while the very same story will leave the very next group of trainees looking at you as though you had suddenly started speaking to them in a foreign language. If this does happen to you, don't be discouraged. A 'good group' can be an amazing experience where everything will seem to go exactly as you planned, but you never know when that next good group will come along. It may also help to realise that, although each group has its own set of dynamics, this doesn't necessarily make training more difficult. We are dealing with people here, so there are always certain similarities.

Similarities

Similarities can be found in all groups of trainees, in that they are all either scholars, or students, or adults, or librarians, or some other type of learner; and each of them will share some very broad characteristics. One of these characteristics is the way in which they learn and, according to Stolovitch and Keeps (2003), most people learn best under the same types of conditions. These conditions include situations where they are able to:

- *See what's in it for them.* If the trainees don't see the purpose of the training from their own point of view, the likelihood of learning is decreased.

- *See a logical order to the material being taught.* If they cannot perceive some sort of order, they can very easily get lost and confused.

- *Get actively involved and practise the tasks set.* When trainees practise something themselves, it makes the process easier to remember than if they had merely watched someone else demonstrate it.

- *Interact with the trainer.* Interaction is usually an indication that the trainees are paying attention.

- *Discuss something with one who knows more than they do about the topic.* Discussion implies some sort of involvement and therefore interest on the part of the trainees.

- *Attend relatively short training sessions.* People have notoriously short attention spans. It seems that people tend to lose concentration after about 20 minutes unless they make a concerted effort, and such an effort can be very tiring.

Stolovitch and Keeps (2002) also speak of people having difficulty learning when too much content is presented at once. In the normal course of events, the human brain is able to filter out most of the stimulation it receives. Consider the example of people sitting and working in an office. Their senses will be bombarded with hundreds of different sights, sounds, smells, physical feelings, and even tastes. Rather than allowing sensory overload, however, the brain merely ignores the unimportant stuff like the traffic sounds and the air freshener smells so the people may instead concentrate on their work.

In other words, the brain does an excellent job of filtering out what is not needed. So it stands to reason that if there is too much content in a training session, each person's brain will quietly go into filter mode and a whole lot of the content will be effectively lost. In addition to this, if the trainees decide they have no need to learn what is being taught, they will consciously ignore a lot (if not most) of the content. The onus is on you as the trainer, therefore, to make sure that there is not too much content for the trainees to learn, and that they themselves feel the need to learn. In order to get them to feel this need, you need to have a very good idea of their attitudes and abilities.

Attitudes and abilities

All trainees bring their own set of attitudes and abilities to a training situation, and you need to have at least a basic idea of what these are. Molberg (2003) states that in order to know one's trainees one should look at things like:

- *Prevailing mood.* Does the training take place on the first day after a long vacation, for example, or during the final class period on a Friday afternoon?

- *Prior knowledge, experience and skills.* If you are going to be using a web-based programme, will the trainee know what you mean when you ask them to follow the link, for example. It is also a good thing to be aware that most people will resist being told something they think they already know.

- *General attitude to the training topic and to learning.* Sadly, in my experience, not many trainees see library research skills as the most exciting thing to learn so we need to make a particular effort here.

- *Group particulars.* For example, age. Adults need a slightly different approach from the one you would take for teenagers.

- *Whether or not English is the second language of the trainees.* You always need to keep your language simple, but extra care is needed when training those for whom English is a second language. It can be very easy to confuse or even to offend. For example, I was a bit puzzled a couple of years ago to keep hearing about a website called 'Amaisin' – pronounced to rhyme with 'raisin'. I have since discovered that what was being referred to was 'Amazon', the online book store. In the same way, the way in which I pronounce certain words has sometimes caused no end of confusion. Having your keywords in written form always helps in cases like these.

- *Learning styles.*

Learning styles

Ever since Kolb (Delahoussaye, 2002) started talking about learning styles in the 1960s, there have been those who agree with the theories and those who do not. Some say that it is impossible to measure someone's learning style with any degree of accuracy, while others refer to specific tests that they say have measured learning styles very successfully. Some researchers have even pointed out that individual learning styles can change with time and circumstance. An approach that works for one person today may, they state, fall sadly flat in the future. It has also been argued that some topics just have to be taught in a certain way, so you cannot cater for different learning style preferences.

I am not sure I agree that certain topics have to be taught in a specific way because I have usually been able to alter the way in which I deliver any lesson in order to better suit the trainees. The occasion that stands out in my mind as an illustration was when I was training a group of design and fine arts students. I had previously had great success with a training programme, but it just did not seem to work when I tried it with these students. They seemed bored to tears by the logical step-by-step approach that I was taking in trying to teach them research skills. In fact, one student asked if he and some of his friends could go and quickly hand in an assignment and, when I gave permission, 12 students left to hand in that assignment and never returned. So I threw out my carefully designed PowerPoint slides and took a problem-based approach in the very next class. Happily, this approach was a great success. Of course, I have since discovered that it would have been easier for me to take note of the learning styles of the design students before I started training.

Another good illustration of this point comes from outside of the library world from a colleague in South Africa:

> My best ever training experience happened in a tiny village near King Williams Town. I had 19 participants on a course and our training room was a tin shack with a dung floor. The walls were so rusted that I couldn't use presstick to attach paper to the walls. When I knelt down on the carpet (that covered the dung floor) fleas jumped onto the paper. I couldn't use words at all, when I recorded stuff on flipcharts, because the participants couldn't read. So I drew pictures instead. The entire training programme was illustrated – I'd never done it like that before. What made the course so great was that despite the many challenges that we had, the participants were anxious to learn as much as they could and they never stopped asking questions and clarifying what they understood. They were the most eager students I have ever encountered and I consider that course one of the highlights of my career. (Susie Spies – environmental education trainer, South Africa)

It seems to me that, regardless of the topic, with a little imagination and lots of enthusiasm you can cater for any learning style.

Neurolinguistic programming model

The model of learning styles that is the easiest to understand is that of Bandler and Grinder (Allan, 2003). Their model of communication uses the neurolinguistic programming

(NLP) styles of auditory, kinaesthetic and visual learning. The auditory learner is the type of person who may forget your face after a first meeting but they will usually remember your name. This person will enjoy dialogue and discussion, and much prefers verbal instructions. In order to make the auditory learner more comfortable, therefore, you should include explanations, as well as provide the opportunity to talk (like in group activities) in your training sessions.

The kinaesthetic learner, on the other hand, is the person who writes down a word to see how it should be spelled. This person prefers to do things rather than talk about them, so your training session should include hands-on and problem-solving sections. Actually, if you believe in that ancient Chinese proverb 'Tell me and I'll forget, show me and I may remember, involve me and I'll understand', then you would be including lots of hands-on and problem-solving anyway. The final type of learner in the NLP model is the visual learner who is the type of person who will remember your face after a first meeting, but will be hard pressed to recall your name. This learner prefers face-to-face interaction and responds well to lots of diagrams, images, videos and demonstrations.

Some of you may recognise certain aspects of all three of these learning styles as being present in your own learning behaviour. As individuals we do not usually fit neatly into a single style to the total exclusion of the others. We tend to lean more towards one type and show certain characteristics from one or both of the other types. Figure 2.1 sets out the differences between the three types. What you have to do is read the word in the left column and then see under which column your answer is most likely to fall. This can give you a very good indication of your own predominant learning style.

Figure 2.1   Find your learning style

When you...	Visual	Auditory	Kinaesthetic and tactile
Spell	Do you try to see the word?	Do you sound out the word or use a phonetic approach?	Do you write the word down to find if it feels right?
Talk	Do you dislike listening for too long? Do you favour words such as see, picture, and imagine?	Do you enjoy listening but are impatient to talk? Do you use words such as hear, tune, and think?	Do you gesture and use expressive movements? Do you use words such as feel, touch, and hold?
Concentrate	Do you become distracted by untidiness or movement?	Do you become distracted by sounds or noises?	Do you become distracted by activity around you?
Meet someone again	Do you forget names but remember faces or remember where you met?	Do you forget faces but remember names or remember what you talked about?	Do you remember best what you did together?
Contact people on business	Do you prefer direct, face-to-face, personal meetings?	Do you prefer the telephone?	Do you talk with them while walking or participating in an activity?
Read	Do you like descriptive scenes or pause to imagine the actions?	Do you enjoy dialogue and conversation or hear the characters talk?	Do you prefer action stories or are not a keen reader?
Do something new at work	Do you like to see demonstration, diagrams, slides, or posters?	Do you prefer verbal instructions or talking about it with someone else?	Do you prefer to jump right in and try it?

Figure 2.1 Find your learning style (*cont'd*)

Put something together	Do you look at the directions and the picture?		Do you ignore the directions and figure it out as you go along?
Need help with a computer application	Do you seek out pictures or diagrams?	Do you call the helpdesk, ask a neighbour, or growl at the computer?	Do you keep trying to do it or try it on another computer?

© Grammatis, 1998. (Used with permission from the author).

The Felder and Silverman model

Brandt (2002) and many others tend to see the NLP model as being a bit simplistic. If you agree with this point of view and need a model with a bit more substance or depth, then the Felder and Silverman model would be a good one to pursue. Tittel (2004) describes this model of learning as one that divides learners into five categories. In each category the learner may lean towards one side of a continuum, but will not usually fall at one end to the total exclusion of the type at the other end.

According to Tittel (2004), the Felder and Silverman model categories are:

- Sensing and intuitive learners:
  - Sensing learners are practical people who like to learn facts. They prefer well-established methods and procedures.
  - Intuitive learners are innovative people who like the discovery of theories and meaning. They don't like repetition.

- Visual and verbal learners:
  - Visual learners remember best the things they see, for example, pictures, diagrams, flow charts and demonstrations.
  - Verbal learners prefer written and spoken explanations. Interesting to note here is that, in their efforts to understand, this type of learner may actually disrupt a training session.
- Active and reflective learners:
  - Active learners prefer to learn by trying things out. They like group work.
  - Reflective learners prefer to learn by thinking about things. They also like working alone.
- Sequential and global learners:
  - Sequential learners are orderly, logically minded people who learn best in small linear steps.
  - Global learners are holistic, systems thinkers, who learn best in leaps and bounds.
- Inductive and deductive learners:
  - Inductive learners prefer to proceed from the specific to the general.
  - Deductive learners prefer to go from the general to the specific.

If you look at the Felder and Silverman categories, the design and fine arts students mentioned earlier in this chapter become very much easier to understand. I have found these students tend to lean towards being intuitive, visual and active learners. In other words, creative, innovative and visually-oriented young people who want to try things out for themselves, and who really get turned off by repetition and procedure. It's no wonder that a logical step-by-step training programme sent them running out of the room at the first opportunity!

When it comes to deductive and inductive learners, it has been found that deductive learners start with the rule and work out problems from there, while inductive learners work back to the rule from the problems. In order to reach the deductive learner, therefore, you should talk in detail about the rules and then provide a relevant problem. Inductive learners, on the other hand, prefer to hear about the problems in detail, while being given the opportunity to describe the rules in their own words. If you have to train students how to use the library catalogue, for example, you can provide for the deductive learners by starting with the rules of the catalogue, explaining what can and cannot be done, and then getting them to use a basic search to find library material. For the inductive learner, you could then go on to approach advanced searching by setting the task before giving any explanations. Just bear in mind that we often tend to follow our own learning styles when designing a training course.

Catering for different learning styles

So how do you know which trainees prefer which learning styles? Well, there are plenty of useful tests available on the Web, and you can pre-test your trainees if you think it necessary. Sometimes, however, the librarian gets to see the trainees only once, so there wouldn't be enough time to conduct pre-testing of this kind. Rather than getting bogged down by all the different learning style models, what is really important here is an awareness of all these learning styles. When you are aware that different people learn in different ways, it is easier to introduce the variety that makes for successful training sessions.

Training sessions should then include, at the very least, hands-on exercises and problems, plenty of graphics, and numerous demonstrations and examples. It is useful to sum up what has been learned in each section, as this can help provide a larger picture and place the training in context. Using all these different approaches can only serve to make your training more lively and interesting. It also helps never to forget that learning should be fun, even if the topic is dull and boring.

Adult trainees

Even adults, whose training needs are different from those of college students, for example, need to have fun when learning. Training adults can, in some ways, be very similar to training young adults or teenagers in that they are ready to learn only what they think they need to learn. Like all other trainees, the adult learner will also want to know 'What's in it for me?' although they do bring a much wider base of experience into the training sessions with them. This experience can be utilised during the training to make for some very interesting and lively interaction.

Adults usually attend training because they need the skill being taught, like lecturers needing to be able to use the new library website in their quest to find online journal articles. Often, however, all their experience, coupled with their age will make the adult learners extremely vulnerable to a loss of face. I have seldom met lecturers who wish to be trained with their students. They seem to feel this may be an indication that they know less than their students, which also makes it difficult for them to ask questions during the training. It may also have a lot to do with status and respect in some cultures.

Adults also tend to view any mistakes they make during training very personally, which can arouse extreme frustration. I remember watching a trainer bravely withstand a verbal tirade from a trainee who was feeling very insecure. She couldn't seem to grasp the reasoning behind the trainer making us perform certain tasks, and she kept on telling him that he was doing it all wrong. The trainer listened calmly and attentively to her woes and explained his methods a number of times in various different ways, all the while treating her with the utmost respect. She wasn't totally convinced but she did settle down and apply herself to the tasks, with no further disruptions to the class. Neither brusqueness nor sarcasm would have defused this situation with as much success. That would have merely made the trainee more anxious and insecure and ultimately more disruptive.

Unlike their younger counterparts, adult learners place a great deal of importance on the state of the learning environment, demanding both physical and psychological comfort. With adult trainees it may be a good idea to carefully observe their comfort levels and perhaps call for breaks more often. You just need to remember to factor these breaks into your overall training time. Adult learners also bring with them very definite expectations about the training, so it would certainly be a good idea for both you and your adult trainees to state your expectations at the beginning of the session. As a final note about adults, they like to take charge of their learning and need to feel that they have a choice in the training sessions.

The element of CHOICE is crucial! Always provide the element of choice when you need to engage the participants in any learning activity, even the simple choice of being there for the training. (Eng Mui Hong – manager, learning and development, Singapore)

One way to give adult trainees the feeling of being in charge is to give them the opportunity to participate in the form of hands-on exercise, discussions and perhaps even the odd game or two.

Active learning

Lots of participation is what active learning is all about. Higher education used to be seen as the pouring of knowledge into empty vessels, but it is becoming very clear that this is not the case at all. Learning improves when people are given the opportunity to ask plenty of questions, hold discussions, and apply and consolidate their new knowledge. In other words, they need to take an active part in the learning process. Active learning, also known as 'learning by doing', makes use of the principle that you learn a skill best when you are allowed to think about it and then practise it. This is very logical when you think about it. After all, what makes a good actor, for example? Years of practice and experience of course! Just consider the case of Clint Eastwood and the difference between his acting in the spaghetti westerns all those years ago and his more recent movies. You could say that practice makes perfect.

When it comes to practice, however, sometimes there may be an initial reluctance to participate on the part of students. Some trainees may prefer to sit quietly and listen to what they are being told, because this is what they have become used to doing. Of course, we seldom experience this kind of reluctance when the trainees are seated in front of a computer because then they usually expect some form of hands-on activity. With the increasing popularity of the problem-based learning approach, our trainees are getting more and more comfortable with the idea of taking an active part in their learning. In fact, sometimes it can be quite difficult to get them to stop taking an active part and listen to what you are saying instead.

Active learning can be implemented very easily during training in the following manner:

- *Give the trainees a task.* Ask them to find books on an obscure topic, for example.

- *Get them to work together in pairs or in small groups.* The really good thing here is that the faster trainees are less likely to get bored as they often end up helping the ones who are slower to understand. You should, however, set a time limit to keep things on track.

- *When the time is up, ask them what they found.* You need to show the trainees how you would have conducted the search using the advanced search options and Booleans or whatever fits in with your training objectives.

Gathering the information you need

Gathering the necessary information about your trainees can be done in a number of different ways. Some of these methods can be extremely time consuming, but it all adds to the preparation that helps you feel more confident and comfortable. It can also help identify the trainees' prior levels of learning because you do not want to present material with which they are already familiar. The best data are normally gathered using a combination of the different ways outlined below:

- *Speak to the lecturers or tutors if students are involved.* These are the people who will have had far more contact with your trainees, and who usually know them better than you do. Even negative comments can be valuable. For example, lecturers telling you that they dread teaching a certain class because the students are so rowdy can give you an indication of what to expect. Incidentally, if you are fortunate enough to have access to remote control software like NetOp (*http://www.netop.com/*) it can be very handy. When I was warned about a group of unmanageable students, I allowed these potentially rowdy trainees to electronically chat, send mail and just generally make a noise while waiting for the session to begin. I then took control of their computers using the NetOp software and made a huge joke of the power I had to force them to pay attention. The students responded very well and I had no problems during the rest of the session.

- *Rely on past experience, either yours or that of a fellow trainer.* Never underestimate the amount of useful advice and help you can get from someone who has already dealt with the type of people you will be training. For example, if you are told that a certain type of group will not answer questions, no matter how many are asked, you can then decide either to scrap all questions as they may be mostly reflective learners, or you can start with very simple questions and leave a longer wait time (i.e. the time in which we wait for a question to be answered). In a recent workshop that I attended, the trainer gave us a charming way of ensuring that our wait time was long enough. This trainer told us to chant the children's nursery rhyme

'Mary had a little lamb' silently to ourselves. It was found that trainers normally average a few seconds' wait time, and this rhyme stops us from moving on too quickly. For those of you who have never heard of this little Western children's ditty, any rhyme that will take you at least 20 seconds to recite will also do the trick. I have personally tried this and it does work, even though to stand in silence for such a seemingly long time can be a little nerve-wracking.

- *Interview the trainees.* You could conduct formal or informal interviews to find out how much the trainees already know about a certain subject, as well as how they prefer to learn. This kind of needs analysis can be very time consuming but particularly useful in the workplace if you are going to be training a very diverse group of employees. You could test the prospective trainees by setting a task like finding journal articles, and watching how they go about the task. Problem areas will be highlighted almost immediately. Finding students who have the time to be interviewed in colleges or universities, however, may present bigger problems and is not usually feasible.

- *Test the trainees.* This type of analysis can be loads of fun as there are a myriad of tests available on the Internet. For example, the *Index of Learning Styles Questionnaire* by Barbara A. Soloman and Richard M. Felder from the North Carolina State University (*http://www.engr.ncsu.edu/learningstyles/ilsweb.html*) or the *Learning Style Survey for College* by Catherine Jester of the Diablo Valley College (*http://www.metamath.com/multiple/multiple_choice_questions.html*). Alternatively, you can use a hard copy, such as the survey in Appendix A. These tests will give you a general idea of the learning styles of your trainees, and can be useful as an awareness raising exercise.

- *Use survey forms.* Some people have advocated the use of survey forms, anonymous or not, to get more of an idea of your trainees. You may, however, have a problem with the response rate unless you physically hand out the forms and wait for them to be completed. You could, of course, mail out vast amounts of the forms, but this may take time and money that you do not have. I am not convinced by this idea, however, as the trainee could just use the form to tell you what you want to hear. An interview would be far better, because then you can watch how the prospective trainees actually behave and so get a truer indication of their skills.

- *Gather data from past reference desk queries, or other patron queries if you will be conducting library training.* Queries made by your patrons can provide a very good sense of the areas in which they are experiencing problems. (See Appendix C for Frantz's article on using questions asked at the library reference desk as the basis for information literacy instruction). If you receive lots of questions on how to find newspaper articles online, for example, you may need to include LexisNexis training in your session. A while back, we were testing some software in the library because we were thinking about providing a virtual reference service. What I found to be the most interesting aspect of this software was the fact that it allowed us to remotely monitor our patrons as they conducted searches on the library catalogue. A lot like spying perhaps, but being able to watch unobserved as the patrons typed in their keywords, was a most illuminating experience for me. I found that the patrons would type in a single word and, when the system returned no hits, they would simply add another keyword to the word already entered. As a result, the system would conduct a Boolean AND search and still return no hits. In my very next training sessions I included a detailed explanation of why this kind of search method always fails to yield results.

There are pros and cons to all of the methods of analysis mentioned above in terms of time, anonymity, objectivity and so on. For instance, if students tell you that they have already been taught a specific topic, you may need to make absolutely sure that they have actually learned something. I have watched many students struggle with concepts that they are supposed to have been previously taught. Remember, sometimes students will say anything if they think it will get them out of library training!

Training is merely another form of the communication process – the process being made up of three basic parts: the sender, the receiver and the message. You as the trainer are the sender of the message, the trainees are the receivers, and the message is contained in your training programme. The onus is on you, therefore, as the trainer to see that the trainees 'get the message'.

The thing to remember about the analysis stage is that it is supposed to give you a better understanding of your trainees. The more you know about them, the easier it will be for you to facilitate learning. What we are aiming for is learner-centred training where the emphasis is on the trainees and their needs, and not on the trainer. We would do well to bear in mind the words of Socrates at this stage, as Triffie Vorster, a customer services manager in South Africa so kindly reminded me:

> Teaching is not a matter of something being placed in one person by another, but one of eliciting something already present.

In other words, the more you know about your trainees, the easier it will be to elicit what is already present.

Motivation

There are few tasks in this world more difficult than trying to teach someone who does not want to learn. One of the biggest problems that we face as librarians is how to motivate students enough to get them to want to learn about the library, as many of them feel they have far more important things to learn. I have found that it helps to follow the ARCS model of motivational design (Small, 1997). John M. Keller came up with the ARCS model in the early 1980s when he identified four elements necessary for the design of instruction that motivates learning:

- *Attention*. Grab the attention of the students by doing something different, surprising or new. For example, instead of explaining and demonstrating how to use the OPAC, start off by asking the students how they would use OPAC to find a specified item. Make it a race to see who will find the call number of the item first.

- *Relevance*. Make the objectives of the lesson very clear from the outset, ensuring that the students can see what is in it for them. Relate what you are training to an upcoming assignment.

- *Confidence*. Always allow time for the students to practise a newly learned skill, and don't present challenges that are too difficult. Make sure any feedback given is positive and make the learning experience fun.

- *Satisfaction*. If you give students examples of topics to search for information on, make sure that there is actually information available. It may sound like superfluous advice to give a librarian, but you must always test any examples that you want to set. Not being able to find any information when students first encounter a database, for example, will hardly entice them to use that database again. Provide plenty of positive reinforcement.

What tasks to include

Once you have a fair idea as to the nature of your trainees and their needs, it is time to look at what they need to learn. For library staff this can usually be answered pretty easily. New students, for example, need to know how to utilise the library to search for and use information in their assignments and projects. If you have recently installed a new library system, or subscribed to a new database, patrons will need to know how to use them. Alternatively, lecturers will approach you with specific training requests like advanced searching for journal articles. Your training sessions may even be part of a course syllabus, with standards and competencies already in place, making it a cinch for you to formulate your list of tasks.

When you know what you will be training, you can break up the content into smaller tasks. So a basic library research skills programme would typically consist of the following tasks:

- accessing the library web page;
- locating OPAC;
- using the OPAC basic search option;
- locating the online databases;

- using the online databases to find journal articles;
- searching the Web effectively;
- evaluating information; and
- citing references.

Delivery options

You will also need to decide how you will deliver your training. Some libraries are fortunate to either have their own, or at least access to, training rooms that are fully equipped with network-connected computers, projectors and screens, and lots of useful software. Others are not so lucky. You need to look at what facilities are available to you and then decide if your sessions will be face-to-face in a classroom, hands-on in a workshop, lecture-style in a larger room, or self-study style online. Even though it has been shown that training works best when the trainees can immediately practise their newly learned skills, sometimes this is just not possible, and we need to find ways to work with what we have.

Budget and time constraints

Time and money also have their parts to play in training programmes, and while some of us may have plenty of money, often many of us do not have enough time. I recall a past occasion where a lecturer contacted me at three o'clock in the afternoon and expected me to start training his students that very night. Although it almost broke my heart to refuse (I hate to miss out on any opportunity to tell students about the library) there was simply no way I could drop all my other commitments, or find an available training venue for that matter. With experience, librarians can learn to keep certain times of the year relatively free and all the training rooms booked and ready. The start of a semester is usually one of these times.

Most of the time you are given lecture or tutorial periods in which to train the students, so the duration of the training sessions will be fixed. You may find, in a case like this, that what you have decided to include in the session just cannot be squeezed into one session. If you really need to include everything that was in your original plan, you could remove some of the tasks from your delivery and present them as handouts the trainees can take away after the session.

As library training sessions can range from expensive programmes that take a project team a couple of years to prepare, like the online Texas Information Literacy Tutorial (*http://tilt.lib.utsystem.edu*), to a simple show-and-tell style workshop, you need to decide what will fit into your time and budget constraints. The good news is that, with the advent of the Web, you have all sorts of programmes available to you at the touch of a button. In fact, many libraries are making use of the Texas Information Literacy Tutorial (TILT) either as is, or slightly modified. You don't have to start a programme from scratch, you just need to decide which one will work best for you and your trainees.

3

Design: consider the objectives

- Identify your *objectives*.
- Decide on your *overall approach*.
- Create the *lesson plan*.
- Determine the methods of *assessment*.

Once you have a clear picture of your trainees, their needs, and the tasks you want them to perform, it is time to identify your training objectives. Sometimes, however, the difference between aims, goals and objectives can get a bit confusing. If you decide to include aims and goals with your objectives, start with your aims, or those broad statements that reflect the intention of your training, and state what it is that you want to achieve. Words like *understand, appreciate* and *know*, usually feature in your aims. Then work out your goals, based on your aims. Goals, although more specific than aims, are broad statements of what should be accomplished in terms of student learning. Finally, formulate your objectives (sometimes called learning outcomes), or the concrete measures by which your aims are to be achieved.

Objectives

Bloom's taxonomy, although originally published in the 1950s, provides a useful way of classifying educational objectives (a taxonomy being, of course, a system for organising into groups things that share the same basic qualities). Krathwohl (2002) goes into some detail about Bloom's taxonomy and this article makes for very interesting reading if you want a quick and easy way to find out more about the original version. Basically, the taxonomy provides us with a set of guidelines to help categorise the learning objectives and the expected outcomes.

Bloom saw his original taxonomy as being, in part, a measurement tool and a way of making it easier for educators to compare learning goals from different courses and subjects. I imagine that the extent to which you would need to go to work out your objectives within the categories specified by Bloom, would depend largely on your particular institution. You might have to plan your training sessions according to specific guidelines and standards, which may or may not include Bloom's theories.

Krathwohl (2002) also provides details about a revised and much simpler version of Bloom's taxonomy, and includes assessment methods to see how well the objectives were actually met. He goes on to describe an objective as a statement that usually includes a 'noun phrase' and a 'verb phrase'. The noun component consists of the subject matter, while the verb component represents the mental processes involved. A typical training objective could, therefore, be represented as:

the trainee will + verb component + noun component.

The verb component could be:

- define;
- demonstrate two ways;
- describe three ways;

- distinguish;
- evaluate;
- explain;
- formulate;
- identify;
- interpret;
- label;
- locate;
- measure;
- name;
- remember;
- select; or
- solve.

Words like *understand, know, reflect* and *realise* are never to be used for objectives as they are just too difficult to measure with any degree of accuracy. How would you, for example, measure the responses of a trainee who has been asked to 'understand the purpose of a library catalogue'? An objective that would be easier to measure in this case would involve getting the trainee to 'describe the two main uses of the library catalogue', where the library catalogue represents the noun component. In case you are a little curious, two such uses could be to allow patrons to search for specific library material and to allow them to browse for material of a specific type. Your overall aim should be to write objectives that are short, to the point and can be clearly understood.

Using Krathwohl's simple method of formulating training objectives, we could come up with the following:

- the trainee will locate the link for OPAC from the library website; and

- the trainee will use OPAC to find the call number and location of an introductory text on psychology.

Dowling and McKinnon (2002) refer to learning and instructional objectives and state that these objectives have three major components. According to them, all objectives should:

- clearly show what is expected from the trainees;

- give the trainer a precise idea of what to train; and

- highlight what is to be evaluated.

Dowling and McKinnon go on to provide a template for objectives that consists of five elements:

- *Conditions of performance.* The trainees should be told precisely how they should perform the required task. For example, 'Using the OPAC Basic Search option, you will find and write down the call numbers and locations of three language dictionaries in descending order of publication'.

- *Performers.* The performer would usually be *you*, in this case '...*you* will write down the call numbers and locations...'

- *Action verb(s).* For example, 'find' and 'write'.

- *Outcome.* The call numbers and locations of the dictionaries will be written down.

- *Standard of acceptable performance.* The call numbers and locations will be recorded according to publication date, with the latest publications coming first. If the numbers and locations are not recorded in descending order of publication, the answer will be incorrect.

Although Watson (2002) prefers to place the development of objectives within the analysis stage of the ADDIE model, he nevertheless also has a very useful way to formulate an objective. He refers to an instructional objective as consisting of four parts:

- *Stem.* This usually reads as 'The trainee will' or even 'At the end of this session the trainee will'.

- *Performance.* Exactly what the trainee will be expected to do.

- *Criteria.* Going back to the previous objective 'Using the OPAC Basic Search option, you will find and write down the call numbers and locations of three language dictionaries in descending order of publication', the criteria or standard would be to write down the numbers and location in order of publication.

- *Condition.* The condition, in this case, would be to use the OPAC Basic Search option. As Brandt (2002) states, conditions of learning are very important. He uses the example of an objective where the user must demonstrate four ways of scrolling down a web page. You have to set the condition as being something like 'when a web page is longer than 28 lines' because if the page ends above the screen fold, as it's called, you will not be able to scroll down.

When it comes to deciding which of these methods of formulating objectives to use, the choice is entirely up to you. As long as you state exactly what behaviour, skill or type of knowledge is required to accomplish the learning objective, you can use the method that best suits your own needs. Sometimes the way suggested by Dowling and McKinnon, for example, can be a little too detailed to apply to a simple task such as finding the link for OPAC on the library website. And we do need a few very simple objectives like these because, when it comes to training library skills, it is vitally important to make sure the trainees know where to find all the systems you are describing.

The good news for beginners, or those of us who are really pressed for time, is that the Association of College and Research Libraries (ACRL) in the USA has already compiled a list of model objectives for academic librarians. Entitled *Objectives for Information Literacy Instruction: A Model Statement for Academic Librarians* (2005), you can find different competency standards, various performance indicators and their outcomes or objectives. As all library training should be about information literacy, your sessions will include many, if not most of these competency standards, so it should be a cinch to adapt any of their objectives to suit your own needs.

Learning theories

Once your objectives have been laid out, you need to look at the approach you are going to take; this is where you need to look at some more theory. There are countless theories in existence today, so a vast amount of literature is available. This may make things a little tedious, but theories can be extremely useful in that they can serve as a framework to help ensure that you don't leave out any important bits. However, as you are not an academic scholar but a trainer in this instance, you do not necessarily have to get bogged down by one theory to the exclusion of all the others.

There is nothing to stop you from using the theory that makes the most sense to you in a certain situation, and then using another theory for another situation in the same training session. You just need to make sure that you select the right theory for the right situation. The question which arises here, of course, is which theory to use. Like Zemke (2002), I am not going to look at all the possible theories, but rather highlight parts of a few theories that contain some of the more useful ideas for trainers to remember.

Pedagogy and andragogy

As you could be training across a number of different age groups in your library, you need to have at least a basic understanding of the theories of adult and child learning. While the term *andragogy* may not be familiar to some, most people have heard of *pedagogy*, a word that comes from the Greek words for 'child' and 'leading' (Hiemstra and Sisco, 1990).

With pedagogy, the teacher leads the child and, as such, is responsible for how, when and what the child actually learns. The premise is that if the teacher doesn't teach it, then the child has no need to learn it. This makes the child almost totally dependent on the teacher. Adults, until recently, were being taught in exactly the same way. With hindsight, this does seem a little odd, as we all know what happens when you make the mistake of trying to treat an adult like a child! In the late 1960s, however, Knowles started talking about the 'art and science of helping adults learn' (Hiemstra and Sisco, 1990) as opposed to the art and science of teaching children. Thus, the theory of andragogy entered the lists.

According to Smith (1999) the term *andragogy* was originally developed by a German teacher in the early 1800s, but no one outside of Germany paid much attention until the theory of adult education surfaced again almost a 100 years later in 1921. At this time, a report took the view that adult education required a different approach from that of child education. In the Western world it was Knowles, however, who became generally associated with the term, and he based his theory on four basic assumptions about adults (Smith, 1999). These basic assumptions are that adults:

- prefer to work things out for themselves;
- learn better through discussion and problem-solving;
- have life experiences that generate specific learning needs; and
- prefer to learn a skill that they can put to immediate use.

Smith (1999) goes on to pick apart the whole concept of andragogy according to Knowles and raises the argument that, if learning is seen as a process of lifelong development, then adult learning and child learning are exactly the same. This makes it a waste of time to look at a separate theory of adult learning. Rather than just dismissing the theories out of hand, however, I would suggest a more logical approach, as suggested by Zemke (2002) when he refers to the placing of andragogy and pedagogy at the opposite ends of a continuum of good teaching methods. At the one end, the learning is directed by the teacher, while at the other end the learning is directed by the students. As a trainer, you choose your position in relation to either end of the continuum, according to the needs of your trainees.

Gestalt in a nutshell

The Gestalt theory is based on how humans fill in the missing bits to get the big picture (Zemke, 2002). Often we will experience the whole event without having seen all the parts, so the whole that we experience will actually be greater than the sum of the parts. A very simple way to describe this is to look at how a movie works. A movie is actually made up of many separate static images flashing past in rapid succession that, if slowed down, would make for an incomplete and very jerky looking picture. What we perceive, however, is motion that is as smooth as that of real life. Our brains just seem to fill in the gaps to make the whole experience more comfortable for us. In the interests of a more comfortable learning experience, therefore, we can help our trainees fill in the gaps. We can begin the lesson by giving them the big picture or an overview of the whole session.

Social learning in brief

On the other hand, those who adhere to the theory of social learning believe that a learner's behaviour changes according to what they see someone else doing, and whether or not there are positive or negative consequences to this behaviour (Zemke, 2002). If the consequences are negative, the learner is not very likely to repeat the behaviour that was observed. As a trainer it is vital to remember this if you are going to be giving a search demonstration, for example.

Before you try to demonstrate a search to your training audience, you must have first tested the search to ensure that records will be found. An unsuccessful search does not encourage the trainees to use the database you are trying to show them, nor does it engender belief in your expertise. Fumbling around during a demonstration may very well leave your trainees with the impression that either the database is inferior, or that your searching skills leave much to be desired. Remember that your aim is to get positive consequences so the students will repeat your behaviour.

The testing of any training demonstration also needs to be carried out for other reasons. A colleague of mine was recently caught 'red-handed' as it were, when he neglected to test a demonstration for an Internet searching skill workshop:

> ...the module was on evaluating websites, focusing on hoax websites. I was using the example of a government website. So I chose to show them the White House website. While typing in the web address, I accidentally typed in '.com'. To my horror, flashed like in a movie-house, was a porn site! With pop-ups appearing uncontrollably. (Rajendra Munoo – librarian, Singapore)

In the heat of the training moment, my colleague had typed in '.com' instead of '.gov', and was fortunate to have the trainees consider it a huge joke. Needless to say, he has since selected and tested his demonstrations very carefully, even catering for possible typing errors. And for those of you who are wondering what he did after his initial shock, well, the only thing he could think of in his panic was to hit the power button.

A bit of behaviourism

A further theory that provides a very useful tip is that of behaviourism. B. F. Skinner, an American psychologist, explained human behaviour in terms of an individual's response to things that happen in the environment (Zemke, 2002). To put it plainly, if the consequence of a response is good, such as a reward, the behaviour tends to be repeated. If the consequence is bad, such as a punishment, the behaviour stops. So learning occurs as a result of an individual's responses to external stimuli.

Skinner's theories may have been torn to shreds in some circles but the important thing to remember here is the concept of reward and punishment. As a trainer, some form of reward is always useful when trying to reinforce certain types of behaviour. You can use the simple and inexpensive technique of sincere praise or, if your budget is up to it, small chocolates or candies. While on the subject of gifts, it should be noted that although they can introduce the element of fun, it is the reward that leaves the trainee with a sense of accomplishment that does the most to encourage learning. Punishments, or any behaviour which can embarrass or humiliate a trainee, should be avoided altogether.

Cognitivism and conditions of learning

A far more popular approach than behaviourism is cognitivism, which deals with the assumption that a learner classifies and organises new information according to an internal knowledge structure. In line with this, Zemke (2002) talks of 'cognitive maps', and states that each individual has their own unique cognitive map. The implication here for us as trainers, is that we need to make our sessions as varied as possible to cater as far as possible for each person's unique way of dealing with information. As that old English idiom states – variety is the spice of life. In other words, life becomes more 'palatable' if you try to do different things in different ways.

Robert Gagné is said to have started off in the behaviourist camp although he eventually moved over to the cognitivist way of thinking. Gagné's theory of learning describes different types of learning, with each type calling for a different type of instruction. According to the Open Learning Technology Corporation (1996), his five major categories were:

- verbal information;
- intellectual skills;
- cognitive strategies;
- motor skills; and
- attitudes.

Nine instructional events

To my mind the most useful part of Gagné's theory is his outline of the nine instructional events (Open Learning Technology Corporation, 1996) because this outline can be used as a step-by-step guideline for portions of a training session. For example, if one of your educational objectives is to get the student 'to identify the format of an information source from its citation', the instructional steps could be as follows:

- *Gain attention.* Tell the students a story about an ethical dilemma. For example, you are travelling on a train and you notice someone suspiciously sidling up to a person with a rucksack on their back. After a while you realise that this someone must be a pickpocket or, at the very least, up to no good. Ask the students what they would do. After a short discussion, explain the point of the story was ethics and relate it to plagiarism and bibliographies.
- *Identify the objective.* Tell the students that they will be learning to compile a bibliography according to the APA

citation style, the style preferred by their lecturers in this case. Explain that a bibliography is a list of all the works they referred to when writing an assignment, and that not citing a work used is the same as plagiarism. Explain that they need to show the lecturer that they did not only consult books but also web pages, journal articles, videos, etc.

- *Recall prior learning.* Tell the students that their reading lists are actually examples of bibliographies. Show them other examples from journal articles and the like.

- *Present the content.* Show the students how they would cite a book, and explain each part of the citation while emphasising the importance of the punctuation.

- *Guide learning.* Show examples of other sources of information and provide the URLs to a number of relevant websites.

- *Elicit performance (practice).* Ask the students to divide up into their project groups. Provide a number of different sources of information to each group and ask them to compile a bibliography from those sources.

- *Provide feedback.* Collect their work and present an example of one citation from each group. State what is correct and what is not.

- *Assess performance.* Go over what has been learned in the session and highlight the common mistakes that have been made during the exercise.

- *Enhance retention and transfer.* At this point I would make the students take an online quiz to see how much they have learned. I usually keep the scores for in-house evaluation but the class lecturers may need the scores for their own records. It may help if the students see their scores so they can see where they went wrong.

Fourteen principles of learning

In contrast to all these different and sometimes complicated theories of learning, Sivasailam Thiagarajan has come up with 14 very simple principles (Workshops by Thiagi, 2003). He divides these principles into those applicable to all living things, those that apply to all people, and those applicable to adults only; and he believes that every trainer should know them. These principles are outlined below.

Laws applicable to all living things

- *Law of reinforcement.* Remember Skinner and his behaviourism? Well, positive reinforcement encourages trainees to repeat certain behaviours, so make sure there is lots of participation to give you plenty of opportunity to praise or reward. Never tell trainees outright that they are wrong, as this can be embarrassing for them. Always be positive and encouraging.

- *Law of emotional learning.* Trainees remember things better if intense emotions are involved, although we obviously don't want things to become too emotional. Use the element of fun or of surprise, for example, with games or perhaps something totally unexpected.

Laws applicable to all living humans

- *Law of active learning.* Being able to get actively involved in a training session makes it easier for the trainees to learn. Rather than allowing them to sit quietly and watch you, include things like quizzes and allow plenty of opportunity for questions and interaction.

- *Law of practice and feedback.* Remember in Chapter 2 I referred to that old Chinese proverb about involving people so they will understand? Well, the same principle is being applied in this law. If you get the trainees involved with hands-on practice, they will be more likely to understand and therefore to learn. What's more, you need to provide constructive feedback on their efforts.

- *Law of individual differences.* We all have different learning styles so it is important to cater for these differences (see Chapter 2 for the theories on learning styles).

- *Law of learning domains.* If you have tried a particular method of getting your point across and found it to be highly successful, you may be tempted to use that method all the time. Unfortunately this will not always work as different situations call for different approaches.

- *Law of response level.* If you get your trainees to practise basic OPAC searches during the workshop, it is too much for you to expect them to use the advanced OPAC search option when they get their first assignments. They will do what they have been taught.

Laws applicable to all living adults

- *Law of previous experience.* Adults bring a wealth of experience with them into a training session, and you should build upon this experience. Of course, the more you know about your trainees, the easier this will be for you to do.

- *Law of relevance.* Adults tend to learn best when they feel they have a need to know what is being taught. You need to show them exactly what's in it for them.

- *Law of self-direction*. Most adults like to take control of their own learning. Try not to force them to do anything, but rather give them an element of choice.

- *Law of expectations*. Adult trainees have their own expectations about the trainer, their fellow trainees, the content of the session, and the way the session is conducted. How and what they learn during the session will be largely shaped by these expectations. The onus is on you as the trainer to ensure they know exactly what will be coming, and that they don't feel threatened in any way. Be careful not to judge or embarrass anyone.

- *Law of self-image*. 'I am just no good with numbers!' or 'I am too old to learn about computers!' When adults have expectations like these, they become like self-fulfilling prophecies. If I think I can't do it, then I probably won't be able to, because I will have little or no incentive to try. People like this need loads of reassurance, and the opportunity to succeed. Make the first tasks easy to complete, but not so easy that the trainees feel patronised.

- *Law of multiple criteria*. One adult may perform a task and judge themselves to have done well, while another adult will perform the same task in exactly the same way but feel they have performed badly. Adults assess what they have done using their own standards, so you need to provide different ways to succeed. For example, if you ask your trainees to find a journal article on a certain topic, allow for the fact that some trainees may use the EBSCO databases, while others may use the link to e-journals available on your library website. If you want everyone to use EBSCO, you must specify this, otherwise recognise the merits of both methods.

- *Law of alignment*. Adults (and young adults) prefer the training sessions to be closely aligned with the real-life situations in which they will be using the skills learned. If you have a group of police studies students to train, base all the examples and exercises in the session on closely related topics, such as safety and security. Of course, this can cause problems with generic programmes that are supposed to cater for trainees across all your institution's subject disciplines. A live session would be easier in that you can simply change the examples and exercises, but an online programme would need a lot more work. One way to deal with this is to duplicate all the online modules and tailor them according to each subject. This way you still have essentially the same programme, but with slightly different content.

Overall approach and lesson plans

By now you should have a very good idea of what approach you are going to take. You will know who your trainees are, what tasks you are going to ask them to perform, what the learning objectives are, and how you will deliver the training programme. Your next step is to draw up your lesson plan. The less experience you have, the longer your lesson plan will be, because beginner trainers usually need to have it all written down. Appendix B includes three fairly detailed lesson plans from the Temasek Polytechnic Library that my colleagues and I have used at one time or another.

The first plan is aimed at first-year students or freshmen; the second is for third-year or experienced students. The final lesson plan deals with an online programme where the trainer never actually gets to meet the trainees face-to-face. You are welcome to use these three plans and adapt them to suit your own purposes (with credit going to the Temasek

Polytechnic Library, please), but the following should be included in every lesson plan you design:

- duration;
- audience;
- prerequisites;
- description;
- materials;
- handouts;
- objectives; and
- contents.

You should always set a time limit on your programme, and make sure all the tasks take less than the total time allocated. In this way you have time to spend on any problem areas that may surface without having to rush, or you can make your trainees happy by letting them out early. In the lesson plans provided, I have allocated a maximum time limit for each section, and left about ten minutes free. When all goes according to plan and there are no hiccups, I usually find myself letting the trainees go early. Online programmes, of course, don't require these timekeeping methods as the trainees would be using their own time and the pace will vary among the trainees anyway.

Next you need to specify who your audience is, and what they need to know before they can attend the training session. Setting clear prerequisites and ensuring the trainees know what they are *before* they attend the session helps to place all the trainees on a similar level of expertise. Having beginners and experts in the same session may make it difficult for the trainer to strike a balance. For example, how do you keep the beginners happy without boring the experts? In point of fact, one way to deal with this type of situation is to break up the class into groups and get the experts to help the beginners.

A description of the lesson is always useful if you are going to re-use the plan at a later date. A quick glance at the description should tell you if the lesson plan will suit your needs the next time. You also need to know what materials are necessary. If the plan calls for one computer with Internet access for each student and your only training room has been booked out, you will need another lesson plan. A note about any handouts you plan to distribute will help you with your pre-session preparation.

The most important part of the plan consists of your objectives. Remember to keep them short, clear and to the point as this will make the contents of your lesson very much easier to plan. The objectives should not be kept a secret but you may wish to reword them slightly when you present then to your trainees, in order to make them more learner-centred. For example, an objective in your lesson plan could be 'By the end of the training session the student will have learned to differentiate between primary and secondary sources'. Reworded for the trainees, this same objective could read: 'By the end of this session you will be able to identify different sources of information'.

As I have said before, the contents section of the lesson plan will be very much shorter for an experienced trainer because the beginner will want to write everything down – from the approach to take with the attention grabber to the precise point at which to include a quiz. Even if you have loads of experience, you might want to consider documenting as much as you possibly can, so that other people can easily use your lessons. This is useful if you find yourself unexpectedly unavailable at any time.

I have used a problem-based learning approach in two of the lesson plans (beginner and advanced) as I have found this to be the best way to introduce active learning into the training session. I don't go into as much depth with the problems as Macklin (2001) who describes how to use problem-based learning when teaching information literacy, but the basic principles are the same. A problem is given to the trainees and they have to decide how best to arrive at a solution, using the specified resources and either working alone or in groups. Once they have solved the problem, the trainer discusses the various approaches taken. With the simpler problems, like finding out if the library has any books on guppies, you can make it a race to find the answer. This type of approach can be great fun and extremely satisfying, but I would suggest that you consider using it after you have a certain amount of experience under your belt. The reason for the warning is that inexperienced and nervous trainers may find it hard to control the timing or deal with the less predictable outcomes.

Assessment

You will notice that I have included quizzes throughout the online lesson plan. These quizzes are very useful when the trainees are learning by themselves and actually serve two functions:

- *To change the pace.* Trainees get tired of passively reading the screen and a change of pace can help keep up the interest levels.

- *To reinforce learning.* Multiple choice, true or false questions, or drag and drop activities introduce the active part into the training and help the trainees think about, practise and remember what they have learned.

Having immediate access to the answers is also very useful as it helps the trainees check their knowledge and make corrections if necessary. Recently, when I was trying out a newly discovered online tutorial, I found myself getting irritated by the fact that the quiz did not show me which questions I had answered incorrectly. When it comes to any form of assessment, we need to know where we have gone wrong in order to learn not to make the same mistakes the next time.

You can provide immediate feedback by using very simple JavaScript coding in HTML pages to create multiple choice options or those questions that require true or false responses. Just search any reputable web browser using the keywords 'free javascript' and you can gain access to thousands of bits of code, tutorials or even to websites that generate the code for you, according to your own requirements. You simply submit your requirements and then copy and paste the results into the HTML code of your web page.

Of course, with authoring software like Macromedia Flash, you can get far more creative with the quizzes. You can add colour, images, and far more interactivity with actions like drag and drop. To make our lives even easier, for those of us who cannot use Flash, there is a wonderful software program called Hot Potatoes which is available free of charge to 'those working for publicly-funded non-profit-making educational institutions' (*http://web.uvic.ca/ hrd/halfbaked/*). With it you can create all sorts of little interactive quizzes, including crossword puzzles, to use in your online web-based training programmes.

At this stage in the development of your training programme, you can also decide what other forms of assessment you wish to include. I usually incorporate a test assignment at the end of all my programmes which tries to ascertain how much the trainees have actually learned. By referring to my objectives, I can quite easily create a number of questions for this purpose. My institution also requires that our trainees reach a certain level of satisfaction, so I include short user satisfaction surveys as well. Once, in an effort to make things simpler for the trainees, I combined both the test assignment and the survey in an online tutorial, but I received a number of complaints, so now I keep the survey separate. Some trainees are just not interested in completing the survey as they don't see the point. They only want to learn and then be tested to receive their grades – anything else strikes them as a waste of time. Fortunately, most of the online trainees actually like to have their say, and I use bribes (small gifts) during the live training sessions.

Development: create the course

- Look at what *others* have done.
- Review your *objectives*.
- Review your *lesson plan*.
- Decide on your *delivery method*.

At this stage of the instructional design process you should be able to state who, why and what you will be training, so now would be a good time to get on to the 'how'. To kick off the development stage of the ADDIE model, my advice would be to start by looking at what other librarians have been doing. Journal articles and books, of course, will give you an idea of what training programmes are out there, as well as how they have been implemented and received. You can have a look at Appendix C for a very short annotated bibliography of journal articles to get you started. The quickest way, however, to find tutorial or workshop content is to type 'information literacy tutorials' into a search engine like Google.

Although most of the tutorials that you will find on the Web will be in the online, distance education format, I find that their content can provide some very good ideas about what to include and how to approach your own sessions – even if your session is going to be live. There is an enormous amount of material available, ranging from programmes that are mostly text-based to those that make use of lots of animation, images and colour. To get you started, I have included below some prime examples of the more interesting tutorials that I have come across.

Please note that some of the URLs provided may have changed since I last accessed them. If you find this has happened and you are still interested in trying to find the tutorial, you can always look for an alternative link on the respective library websites. For example, for *http://www.library.unisa.edu.au/infogate/* just remove the '*infogate/*' portion of the URL. I should also like to point out that I was investigating these tutorials as a member of the public and may not, therefore, have had access to some of the features. For example, in cases where I could not find a quiz, the institution may have other provisions for assessment in place. If you are going to be looking at these tutorials with a view to developing your own, I would suggest that you contact the librarians concerned for more in-depth information.

A business-like approach with extras

The online tutorial *Seven Steps to Effective Library Research* from the Olin and Uris Libraries of Cornell University in the USA (*http://www.library.cornell.edu/olinuris/ref/research/tutorial.html*), uses very simple HTML pages. In my personal opinion, the format used is a little too reminiscent of the old printed library handouts. I believe that the Web, with all its hyperlinking, animation and imaging capabilities, should not be used like a simple word processor. In addition, the navigation of this online tutorial can be a little confusing at times, but it should be remembered that the content is aimed strictly at university-level researchers. With this particular audience in mind, the tutorial takes a business-like, no-nonsense sort of approach and covers all the essential elements of information literacy under the following sections:

- deciding on a topic;
- looking for background information;
- finding books;
- finding journal articles;
- finding information on the Internet;
- evaluating the material; and
- citing the sources.

What I really like about the tutorial is its three short and very informative video demonstrations. These video clips show the students how to search for books, video and sound recordings; as well as how to conduct quick and easy or in-depth searches for journal articles. The clips do a lot towards making it easier for those whose learning styles lean towards the visual and the auditory. As attention grabbers, they also introduce a change of pace. Viewed with RealPlayer or QuickTime players that are freely available on the Internet for download, these demonstrations make use of screenshots of the library catalogue and databases, with verbal instructions and animation that shows the cursor movements, drop-down menus and so on. Figures 4.1 and 4.2 show the title screen and an example of the content of this online tutorial.

Figure 4.1	*Seven Steps to Effective Library Research* from the Olin and Uris Libraries at Cornell University

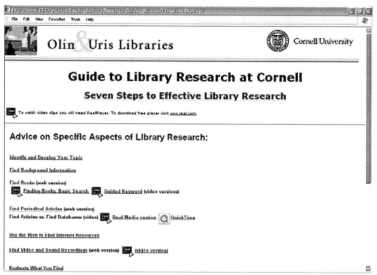

© Reference Department; Instruction, Research, and Information Services (IRIS); Cornell University Library; Ithaca, NY, USA (used with permission).

Figure 4.2	Example content from *Seven Steps to Effective Library Research*

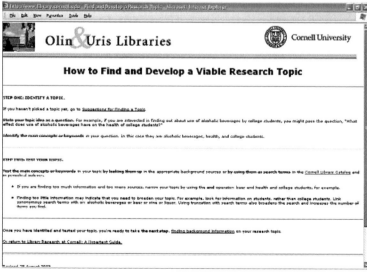

© Reference Department; Instruction, Research, and Information Services (IRIS); Cornell University Library; Ithaca, NY, USA (used with permission).

Inspiration from Ireland

The University of Limerick in Ireland (*http://www.ul.ie/ libraryquickstart/*) starts off its inspirational library tutorial, *Quickstart: The Library Step-by-Step*, with five useful facts, that is, answers to the questions that all of our patrons usually ask, namely:

1. When does the library close?
2. How do I get help either in person, via e-mail, or on the telephone?
3. Where are the books?
4. How do I borrow library materials?
5. What photocopying services are available?

Adding to the five useful facts, the rest of the sections include information on finding books, subject information, journals and information on the Web. In addition to this, by the time this book has been published, the University of Limerick Library should have another online tutorial available for their patrons – this time dealing with citing references according to the Harvard citation style.

The best part about the *Quickstart* interactive programme is that it uses loads of animation and images, and is very easy to understand with pop-up mini-tutorials that require the students to think, click, type and generally get involved in the learning process (active learning). The mini-tutorials also try to engage the attention of the students by requiring them to click on certain areas of the screen in order to move forward. The title screen makes use of the mouse roll-over effect, so when the patron's cursor rolls over certain parts of the diagram of the library, different explanatory text appears, the library doors open and so on.

Figure 4.3 The *Quickstart* title screen, showing a cut-away image of the library

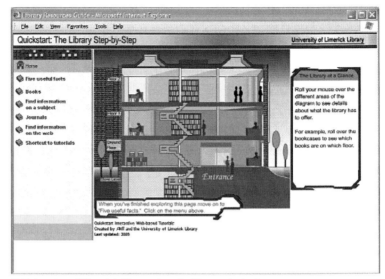

© University of Limerick Library (used with permission).

Figure 4.4 Example content from *Quickstart*

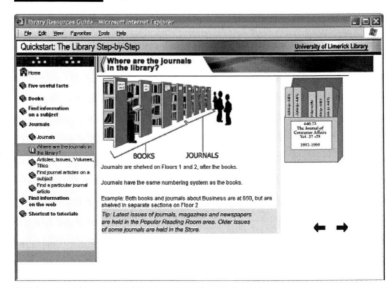

© University of Limerick Library (used with permission).

Figure 4.5   One of the *Quickstart* mini tutorials

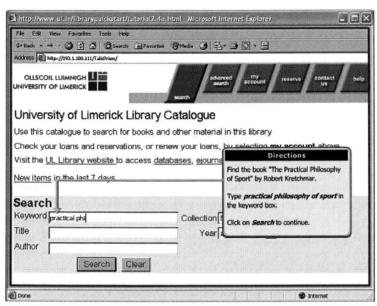

© University of Limerick Library (used with permission).

There is also a navigation menu down the left side of the screen so patrons always know where they are in the programme. Like Cornell University's *Seven Steps to Effective Library Research*, there are no quizzes included. However, there is far less text, and each screen ends before the fold, so the students are not required to wade through too much text or even scroll down. The design is consistent throughout the site, so you can tell immediately when you have left the tutorial. Figures 4.3–4.5 show screenshots of the title screen of this online tutorial, examples of the content and one of the pop-up mini tutorials.

An exciting example for the public

A very nice example of a tutorial from the public library sector is the *Ticket* to *Find* programme at *http://www.tickettofind.org.uk.* A joint effort of the Adult Education Service, the City of Wolverhampton College, the University of Wolverhampton and the Wolverhampton Library and Information Service, this programme looks to bring information literacy skills to the people of Wolverhampton. It also answers the 'What's in it for me?' question very neatly by counting as a one credit course towards higher education access. The course is free, but the learner has to attend the face-to-face sessions in order to receive the actual qualification.

Ticket to Find allows the learner to start the course via one of five entry points, namely, childcare, health, education, neighbourhood and family history. In other words, all those topics that would be of interest to the more mature learner. Navigation is made easy with a consistent design all through the site, a list of module contents to the left of the screen, and a menu bar of links to all the modules near the top of the screen. Each module includes an introduction, a short scenario, a quiz and an example of the assignment that would need to be written if the accompanying lecture is going to be attended.

All the information literacy skills are covered, that is, identifying an information need; searching for and finding information (in this case, from the Web only); and then evaluating, recording and using that information. Quite a bit of white space is used with the text and images and only sometimes will the learners have to scroll down the screen past the fold. The pop-up interactive quizzes present multiple choice questions or crosswords, and provide immediate answers. In my opinion, this online tutorial really merits our attention, especially if we are going to be training adults, and the crosswords are great fun to try.

One of the more well-known tutorials

In the late 1990s, it was decided that the 16 different institutions making up the Texas System Digital Library needed an online tutorial to cater for the information literacy needs of their students (Fowler and Dupuis, 2000). And so the Texas Information Literacy Tutorial, or TILT, was born. Designed to be used on or off campus, and to be compatible with a Macintosh or a PC, Netscape or Internet Explorer, this interactive tutorial even provides a 'lite' version that does not require a Flash player. Learners can register or sign in as a guest and then select an entry point such as 'Censorship and Freedom of Speech' or 'Laws and Regulations' (*http://tilt.lib.utsystem.edu*). From here they get taken through the steps of an introduction to the Internet, selecting and searching for information and then evaluating the information found. The tutorial ends with a closer look at the library the learner will be using to find this information.

TILT makes use of text, images, animation, sound and short quizzes in an effort to engage the learner, with a fun gadget and a gauge that will tilt to green if you answer the question correctly. The other quizzes also provide immediate feedback about your answers. The creamy-yellow background of the site is, for many, slightly more soothing than a glaring white and, although scrolling below the fold is required on many of the pages, there are consistent navigation arrows to go backwards and forwards. Moving around the site is also facilitated by a menu to the left of the screen, and a very useful sitemap that allows you to go straight to sections of your choice. Each section wraps itself up very neatly with a review of the objectives that were outlined at the beginning of each module.

To my mind, however, the best parts of TILT are the guided search sections. Here the tutorial makes use of web page frames to guide the learner through a database search. On a single web page, the one frame has a set of instructions, while the database itself appears in the second frame. In this way, the learner can search the database in the one frame while following the instructions that appear simultaneously in the other frame. This technique is extremely useful for remote database training, but one which will definitely need the permission of the copyright holders of that particular database. As framing someone else's web pages can be almost like gluing your own cover onto someone else's novel, you also need to ensure, like TILT does, that your frame does not appear to claim ownership of the other web page in any way.

The most notable thing about TILT is that other libraries have also found it extremely useful, so the tutorial is now available under open publication licence. This basically means that as long as you give credit to the original creators, you can download and adapt TILT for your own library use. So if you decide to use an online programme, you may find that it better suits your needs to adapt an existing tutorial like TILT. The list below provides examples of a few libraries that have done just that:

- Liverpool John Moores University – LIST (*http://cwis.livjm.ac.uk/lea/info/list/menu1.htm*)

- Southern Connecticut State University –BILT (*http://fred.ccsu.edu/TILT/*)

- University of New South Wales – LILT (*http://www.library.unsw.edu/%7Epsl/itet_lilt/intro/enter.htm*)

- Western Michigan University Libraries – Searchpath (*http://www.umich.edu/library/searchpath/*)

The Australian experience

The libraries of the Queensland University of Technology, the University of South Australia, James Cook University and the University of Technology in Sydney, Australia all have information literacy tutorials that are based on a programme from the California Polytechnic State University (see Figure 4.6). *Pilot*, the Queensland University of Technology Library's tutorial, adapted California Polytechnic State University's framework, content and source code, while *Visa* from James Cook University Library, *InfoGate* from the University of South Australia Library and *Catalyst* from the Sydney University of Technology Library were all adapted from *Pilot*. The tutorial from America is actually made up of what it refers to as nine different tutorials, while the Australian versions have combined nine modules into one tutorial.

Figure 4.6	California Polytechnic State University Library's tutorial title screen

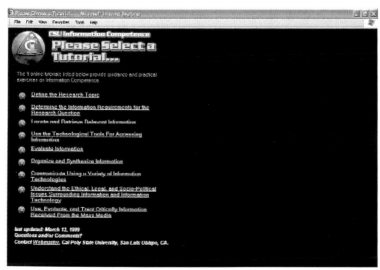

http://www.lib.calpoly.edu/infocomp/modules/index.html
© California Polytechnic State University Library (used with permission).

I was informed by the California Polytechnic State University, in late 2005, that they were in the process of revamping their entire website and making their information literacy tutorial more specifically course-related. I was also given the privilege of being allowed to take a peek at the prototype site, which, if not available as you read this, will be very soon. I found the visual difference between the old black background with its nine separate tutorials and the corporate style approach of the new tutorial with its six modules, quite startling but refreshing.

Pilot and *InfoGate*, which were adapted from the original Californian programme, make use of a pre-test to determine how much the students know before they start the tutorial. If the students obtain more than a certain percentage marks-wise, they are then allowed to skip the tutorial. All four of the Australian tutorials have a glossary and a final quiz, but only *Pilot* tracks the students by getting them to login. The other tutorial quizzes don't keep track of the student participation, or even provide feedback on the student answers, and I found I could move forward in the tutorial by selecting the next button without responding to any of the questions. In my experience, if you do not track the students in some way and make the quizzes compulsory, they tend to skip them to save time. If you are using the quizzes as a way of engaging the students and reinforcing learning, then I think it would be better not to let the students ignore these tests.

Although the tutorials all make good use of white space, images and animations, and have essentially the same content, I found it fascinating to note the visual impact of the different designs – just look at the difference between Figures 4.6 to 4.11. *Pilot* and *InfoGate* (Figures 4.7 and 4.8) have essentially the same title screens, but there is more text on the *Pilot* screen, almost making it appear as if there is slightly more work involved. In fact, when I was asking for

| **Figure 4.7** | Queensland University of Technology Library's *Pilot* title screen |

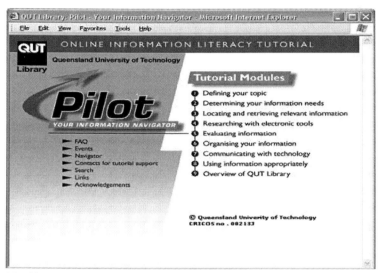

http://www.library.qut.edu.au/pilot/
© Queensland University of Technology (used with permission).

| **Figure 4.8** | The title screen of the University of South Australia Library's *InfoGate* |

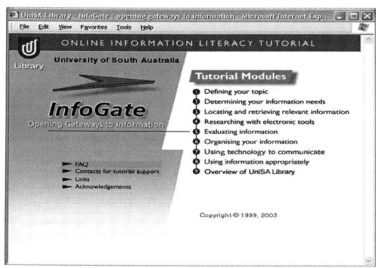

http://www.library.unisa.edu.au/infogate/
© Queensland University of Technology, California State University, James Cook University, and University of South Australia (used with permission).

Figure 4.9 Queensland University of Technology Library's new *Pilot* tutorial

http://pilot.library.qut.edu.au/.
This image was provided from the development site in 2005.
© Queensland University of Technology (used with permission).

Figure 4.10 The *Visa* tutorial title screen from the James Cook University Library

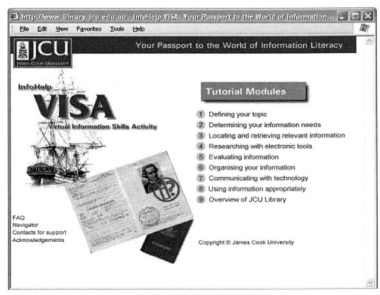

http://www.library.jcu.edu.au/VISA/
© James Cook University (used with permission).

Figure 4.11   *Catalyst* from the University of Technology, Sydney

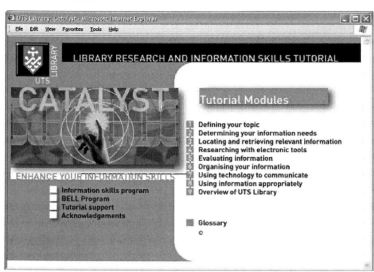

http://www.lib.uts.edu.au/catalyst/
© Queensland University of Technology, California State University, and
University of Technology, Sydney (used with permission).

permission to use these screenshots, I was informed that the Queensland University of Technology would have uploaded their new version of *Pilot* by June 2006 – see Figure 4.9. Their new interface uses less text.

The new *Pilot* tutorial was pared down to six modules from the original eight, partly in an effort to make the programme shorter for their students. At the Temasek Polytechnic Library, we recently designed an online tutorial using eight modules, thinking that this would make the overall navigation easier. The feedback from many of the learners, however, was that the tutorial was too long. When my colleague placed essentially the same content into three modules, the reaction was far more favourable. I suppose as a busy undergraduate the thought of having to work through three modules is easier to cope with than the thought of eight modules, no matter how short those eight modules are.

The word 'Visa' in the *Visa* tutorial (Figure 4.10) comes from the phrase 'Virtual Information Skills Activity' which is then used as a theme – visas and passports to information literacy, with images of ships and immigration documents. Have you ever noticed how we as librarians like to give names to things like our library catalogues and so on? Some people argue that this is not a good idea as it merely gives the learners something else they need to remember and get used to, while others feel that a catchy name is a good memory aid. I personally don't feel very strongly either way here, but I do know that assigning names makes it easier for us as library staff to identify the services we offer and report to management on their effectiveness.

The *Catalyst* tutorial (Figure 4.11) is the most colourful and my personal favourite, as orange is such a young and cheerful colour. If you look at the theories of colour psychology, one of the most often used colours is blue, which is cool and peaceful and is supposed to encourage concentration. Orange, on the other hand, is supposed to make a person feel confident and energetic, which is exactly how you would want a trainee to feel. Just remember that people's reaction to colour is culturally based, so a colour combination that is well received in one country may have negative connotations in another. Black backgrounds, for example, are not usually well received by adults all over the world as black is seen in many cultures as being a sign of mourning.

Figures 4.12 and 4.13 show screenshots of the content from the tutorials of the California Polytechnic State University and James Cook University. Although the Australian screen example from *Visa* has far more content,

Figure 4.12 California Polytechnic State University Library tutorial content

© California Polytechnic State University (used with permission).

Figure 4.13 Tutorial content from James Cook University Library

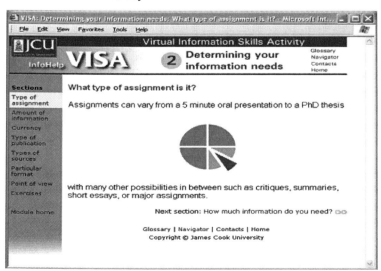

© James Cook University (used with permission).

the learners will always know where they are in the tutorial because of the very clear title and module header at the top of the screen. With all the clicking and linking you go through on web pages, it is very easy to 'get lost' as it were, so online navigation and a consistent design are always important considerations.

The pick of the crop

The TIP programme from the University of Wyoming at *http://tip.uwyo.edu/* is to my mind the most impressive tutorial I have come across so far, probably because it fits in so well with the needs of the Temasek Polytechnic Library. Created by five librarians, a graphic designer and a computer programmer, this tutorial makes extensive use of Flash to provide a colourfully interactive and very useful session. On the negative side, it starts with a Flash introduction, which can get very irritating if you enter the tutorial more than once. In addition, it is designed for a screen resolution of 1024 by 768 pixels, although many people still use the 800 by 600 pixels screen setting. These are pretty minor considerations, however, when the tutorial is part of a credit course so the learners know right away what's in it for them. As I have said before, this is a very important point when trying to motivate trainees to learn.

There are five different sections that include defining a topic, searching for and finding information, evaluating and finally using the information. Each section begins with a real-life personal example of a research need that moves smoothly into an application in the academic situation. For example, the trainees are presented with the situation where they hear a song and need to identify it so they can add it to their own collection. The point is that investigation will find the name of the song or the band and investigation is what needs to be done for assignments and projects.

Another positive aspect is that all the quiz results are available immediately as a percentage and are emailed to the respective lecturers. But the best thing about TIP is that like TILT, it is available under open publication licence so you can grab it to adapt for your own library needs, after having registered and signed the licence agreement, of course. Figure 4.14 shows the Flash entry screen, the only Flash introduction left after feedback from the students on how annoying this type of introduction can be (Phillips and Kearley, 2003). Figures 4.15 and 4.16 show examples taken from the title screen and content of this tutorial.

Figure 4.14   TIP Flash entry screen

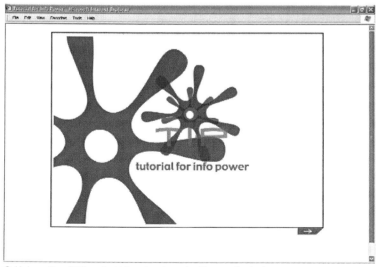

© University of Wyoming Libraries (used with permission).

Figure 4.15 The TIP title screen

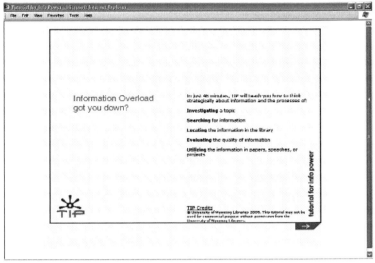

© University of Wyoming Libraries (used with permission).

Figure 4.16 An example of TIP content

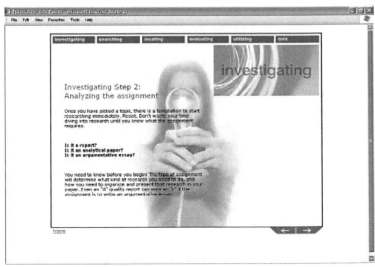

© University of Wyoming Libraries (used with permission).

Review your objectives

After having looked at all the marvellous things your fellow librarians are doing with information literacy training, you may want to review your objectives to make your planned programme longer, shorter, or even slightly different. For example, you may wish to alter your objectives as you may find others that seem to make more sense within your training context. You may wish to split up some objectives into more than one to make them simpler, or you may find that you need to cut down on the number of objectives as there won't be time to include them all.

I often find it difficult to gauge how long a process will take, because the timing will depend on a number of different factors. One group of trainees may work through a lesson very much faster than another group who will seem to struggle with grasping the same concepts. In addition, the more trainees you have, the longer it will take to ensure that they all keep up with you. The network may be particularly slow one day, or it may stop working altogether. This means you will have to use a prepared demonstration, which is always faster to work through than a live one. The time taken by one trainer will also differ from the time taken by another trainer for the same content.

The best advice I can offer for beginners is to see how much time others have budgeted, watch others training or, if this is not possible, practise your own delivery somewhere in front of friends or colleagues, or even in an empty room. Make sure you allocate more time than you think you will need, as it is always better to let the trainees out a bit early than to rush your training. What's more, never assume that if you are given an hour and a half, that you will be able to train for the full 90 minutes. Students, for example, need time to get from one class to the next, so at least 10 minutes of your lesson may be lost.

Review your lesson plan

Once you have investigated the approach taken by existing programmes and perhaps altered some of your own objectives and directions, your lesson plan may also need reviewing. Not all of us are fortunate enough to have our information literacy programmes form part of our institution's curriculum. If your programme is not part of a campus course requirement, to encourage participation, you need to make sure that the content of your session answers the trainees' 'what's in it for me' question. One of the best ways to do this is to relate it as closely as possible to their course work. All the search demonstrations and activities should contain examples that tie in with the topic of the trainees' next assignment – perhaps you can even let the trainees start researching for this assignment in your session. Just make sure that the design of your lesson plan includes activities to help you to reach your objectives.

Ten fundamental design principles

According to Allan (2003), there are ten fundamental principles of design that matter. You need to:

- *Include as many activities and interactions as possible.* You want to engage the trainees to increase the amount of learning that will take place.

- *Make sure the trainees don't get lost by leaving breadcrumbs, or sign posts.* Trainees like to know how much they have left to get through. In a workshop you could provide content outlines, in an online programme each web page could state something like 'page 3 of 15'. Do not, however, include your time estimates for the trainees to see. You may choose to spend more than the allotted time on one section and this may alarm some of the trainees into thinking that the workshop will not finish on time. They then start worrying about getting to their next lecture, for example, instead of paying attention.

■ *Change the pace regularly.* People tend to start losing concentration after a while, so a change of pace every 20 minutes will help to keep your trainees alert and interested.

■ *Divide the content into chunks.* Most people are able to remember 'seven recently learned chunks' of information (Chambers and Associates, 1997) so you need to arrange your content into seven chunks or fewer.

■ *Use the same language and examples the trainees would use.* Do not, however, try to be cool. Always remember that while you can have fun, you are the trainer and you have important information to impart.

■ *Give the trainees choices.* The choice can be as simple as where to sit during the session. Some form of choice will make the trainees feel more in control and therefore more receptive to learning.

■ *Bring up any objections and deal with them.* If the trainees have a problem during the class, try to clear the air before you move on. One suggestion is that you move a disruptive student to the back of the class with the comment that student B is having problems seeing the screen so could the disruptive student please exchange seats. Or you could call for a time out and promise to discuss the problem with the individual after the class. Try to keep calm and do not get sarcastic or embarrass anyone.

- *Strive for a balance of theory and practice.* Your entire session should consist of a balanced mix of your talking and trainee discussion and hands-on practice.

- *Make feedback part of the session.* You need to know what the trainees think of the workshop. A lot of the suggestions may be about things beyond your control, like the number of computers inside the training room, but there are often some very helpful comments.

- *Have a definite ending to the session.* Wrap up the session with a brief summary and perhaps a thought-provoking or interesting quote that is related to the content. I find that asking for questions at the end never works as the students are always in a hurry to get somewhere else.

Decide on your delivery method

At this stage you should have a very good idea of how you will be delivering your programme. You may have the luxury of being able to choose your method of delivery, or you may be constrained by staff numbers, student numbers, or even lack of facilities. Whatever method you use, it is always good to remember that the point of your presentation is to help you to get your message across – not show how brilliant you are at using the latest technology.

Too many bells and whistles may distract the trainees from the actual learning points of the session. To this end, I would suggest you ignore all those bright, interesting web and PowerPoint templates that are freely available on the Internet today. As exciting as they look, they often end up overpowering your content, so it is better to keep your screens and backgrounds plain and simple. Use a bit of colour psychology too. For example, blue in the background which changes to orange when you reach a quiz or other activity for the trainees. Do remember, however, that you need to check the way in which your colours will appear when projected onto the screen in the training room itself. What looks good on your computer screen may become illegible on the projection screen.

PowerPoint slides

PowerPoint slides are probably the simplest way for most of us to produce a colourful session that will help guide us through the content. It can be very easy to forget one's lines when one is nervous, so having the slides with their instructions can be a life-saver. If you are using transparencies and an overhead projector, most of the tips on creating PowerPoint slides will also apply. For PowerPoint, just add notes to each slide and when printing, select in the following order:

- Print What – Handouts.
- Slides per page – 2.
- Print What – Notes pages.

This will give you two slides per printed page and all your notes will be included. During your delivery, you may also find that adding handwritten notes and reminders in different colours will help for your next class.

Images, sound effects and music can all be added to your PowerPoint slides to introduce a change of pace and cater for the different learning styles. If you are using Microsoft Office, the clip art collection is really very good as it offers all kinds of images, photographs and sound clips for your use. This collection can be searched too, making the finding of specific items a cinch. And for those who want to offer something more in the way of animation but cannot use, or do not have access to Flash, a wonderful application from Macromedia called Breeze Presenter was recently brought to my attention. With Breeze Presenter you can create an animated PowerPoint show, record and add verbal instructions and insert interactive quizzes to end up with Flash clips very much like those offered by the Cornell University Library (*http://www.library.cornell.edu/ olinuris/ref/research/tutorial.html*). Breeze Presenter makes the clips very much easier to produce – if you can use PowerPoint, you can use Breeze Presenter.

Important PowerPoint tips

Apart from keeping the background of your PowerPoint slides relatively simple, you might like to keep in mind the following pointers as provided by Wilder and Rotondo (2002):

- *Never read your slides to your trainees.* This is incredibly boring for your audience and not what training is all about. If you want the trainees to read the slides, send the slides via e-mail and let the trainees read them for themselves. What you should do instead is use very short sentences and phrases that remind you what to say, not say it for you.

- *Don't use images unless they tie in with your content.* Putting in a picture because you want a flash of colour will just irritate your trainees and draw their attention away from your content. If you cannot find an image that depicts your point, it is better to use no image at all.

- *Don't use text, bulleted or otherwise, that flies in from 'offstage'.* Having your sentences fly in from the side to make a grand entrance is to me just too much like covering up your next point on the overhead projector with a piece of paper. If you don't want your trainees to see something, don't put it on the slide. I have also watched trainers who skip through the 'flying' section to get all the text on the screen before they start talking. This just makes them look unprepared.

- *Be careful with flying images.* Flying images can also distract and irritate your trainees, although I feel that a judiciously used moving image can attract rather than detract attention. Just don't make your images leap about too often and make sure the animation enhances your content. Slide transitions too, should not be too elaborate. If your whole presentation consists of one slide 'checker boarding' into another the whole time, it can get quite annoying.

- *Don't talk to the screen.* It is very tempting to look at the projection screen when you are training, but if you are talking at the same time; your trainees will not be able to hear you properly. If you can, position the trainer's computer or laptop in front of you so you can look at it instead. Otherwise, stop talking when you point to something on the projection screen. And when it comes to pointing, if you must use a laser pointer, make sure the dot is large enough to actually see from as far back as the last row, and don't shake it around too much. A wobbling red dot will distract attention, not attract it. You could also try using your mouse cursor to point to things onscreen.

- *Keep your slides uncluttered.* Always keep the contents of each screen down to six points or less, preferably making them bulleted points as opposed to whole sentences, and don't use the same word more than five times per screen. Stick to one concept per screen and only one or maybe even two sans serif typefaces, such as Arial or Verdana. Fancy fonts like Bauhaus 93 or Desdemona may look good, but they cannot always be easily read, nor can they be found on all computers. If you design your slides using a fancy font, your whole layout is apt to change on a computer that does not have the same font installed. You can also highlight key words and phrases in bold or with text boxes and put numbers in charts. But when it comes to charts and tables, never include a chart or table that cannot be easily read by the trainees. I have often watched in irritation as trainers or presenters show a table and then tell everyone that they won't be able to read what's in the table. So why waste our time by showing it? Above all, the slides should be neat and easy to read.

- *Use a remote mouse.* This is a difficult one as often we simply don't have access to a remote mouse. Standing behind the desk and clicking the mouse is not ideal and neither is having someone try to move the slides forward for you. Moving behind the desk to push the page forward key and then moving out again is, however, the lesser of the two evils. I recently watched a PowerPoint presentation where a very nervous speaker and helper got themselves terribly mixed up. The helper raced off to the last slide, backtracked, and found the last slide again before the speaker had finished the introduction. The audience ended up laughing at what the helper was doing and not listening to the actual presentation.

Wallace, writing for the Law Library Resource Xchange, approaches the subject of presentations from an entirely different angle (Wallace, 2001). By telling you what to do to *ensure complete disaster*, she suggests that you follow 12 simple guidelines. Well worth reading, I have merely summarised Wallace's ideas from this delightful article:

- Try to suppress all evidence of eagerness when you talk.
- Never look at your trainees during the session.
- Use your body to cover the slides on the screen.
- Attempt to include at least four different typefaces on every slide.
- Try to use as few slides as possible so you don't waste any white space.
- Select the colours you like and don't worry about what they look like onscreen.
- Cover up any remaining white space with your favourite images.
- Always keep your objectives a secret.
- Talk about what you are interested in.
- Test your equipment at the last moment.
- Save paper by not providing handouts.
- Say what you have to say and don't worry about the time limits.

HTML and web pages

Another option is to use web pages for your training presentations. FrontPage and Dreamweaver are very easy to use for those who are not inclined to use hypertext markup language (HTML). You can load a web page onto your institution's server which will allow your trainees to follow along with you in the workshop, as well as have unlimited access to any hyperlinks you make available. In addition, although many of us still provide live library workshops, the trend with shrinking budgets, fewer staff and greater student numbers, is to provide library training online, for which the Web is an excellent medium. You just need to remember to keep your web pages easy to use.

Jakob Nielsen has written extensively on web usability and while I feel he sometimes goes to extremes in his call for simplicity, he has some very useful points to make. I would suggest that, at the very least, you try to avoid the top ten mistakes that were made in 2005 (Nielsen, 2005). These mistakes include the use of font sizes that are too small for some people to read, not underlining the hyperlinks or using the default link colours, and copying the old text-based library guides and bibliographies straight onto a web page. The Web is often treated in the same way as print media with the end result being boring text-filled pages where the patrons have to scroll endlessly to find anything. To me, colour and sound are always welcome on a web page.

Images, animation, sound and music can all be added to your sessions with great ease and Flash is being utilised more and more, although Nielsen (2005) has quite a bit to say against the use of Flash. Flash can be very useful in that you can introduce a much greater level of interactivity, like animated database search demonstrations, or drag and drop quizzes. In fact, our trainees today are such sophisticated Internet users that they almost expect this kind of interactivity. However, those little Flash animations that introduce us to a website are not included in these expectations. Even if you have an option to skip the animation, it merely becomes irritating after a while and should, according to Nielsen, be avoided. The creators of the TIP programme from the University of Wyoming found that most of their trainees agreed with Nielsen too. Flash can also be difficult for some of us to grasp. As I mentioned

Figure 4.17 Code for a simple JavaScript quiz

A

```
<SCRIPT LANGUAGE='Javascript'>
<!--
function answer(ans) {
if (ans == '1a') {alert('No - please try again!');}
if (ans == '1b') {alert('Well done! Journal articles
contain the latest, most up-to-date information.');}
if (ans == '1c') {alert('No - please try again!');}
if (ans == '2a') {alert('No - please try again!');}
if (ans == '2b') {alert('No - please try again!');}
if (ans == '2c') {alert('Yes - the Library catalogue is the
best place to search for information in the Library.');}
}
// -->
</script>
```

B

```
1. What would be a good source for the very latest,
most up-to-date information?
<p>
<input type='button' name='1a' value=' A '
onClick='answer(this.name)'>
        encyclopedias &amp; dictionaries <br>
<input type='button' name='1b' value=' B '
onClick='answer(this.name)'>
        journal or periodical articles<br>
<input type='button' name='1c' value=' C '
onClick='answer(this.name)'>
        books
<p>
<hr width='85%'>
2. The best way to search for information in the library
  is to...
<p>
<input type='button' name='2a' value=' A '
onClick='answer(this.name)'>
        browse among the shelves<br>
<input type='button' name='2b' value=' B '
onClick='answer(this.name)'>
        ask a friend<br>
<input type='button' name='2c' value=' C '
onClick='answer(this.name)'>
        use the library catalogue, OPAC
<p>
```

earlier, Breeze Presenter can be used instead of Flash, but if you don't have access to this application, you can get similar effects using simple JavaScript.

The nice thing about JavaScript is that you can find any number of websites that make portions of this script freely available to all. There are even websites where you enter your requirements and the script is specially generated for you. With JavaScript you can create those roll-over effects where an image will change when the cursor moves over it, or simple interactive quizzes. For example, for a two question multiple choice quiz with three possible answers for each question, simply copy the code from Figure 4.17(a) into the head of an HTML document, and the code from Figure 4.17(b) into the body of the document. This will give you something that will look like Figure 4.18 on your web page.

When the trainee selects an answer button, a small window will pop up with the alert text from the first part of the JavaScript.

Figure 4.18   Simple JavaScript quiz

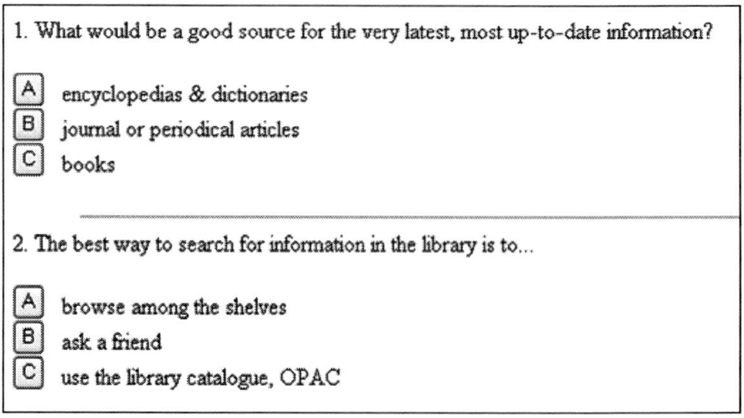

1. What would be a good source for the very latest, most up-to-date information?

   [A] encyclopedias & dictionaries
   [B] journal or periodical articles
   [C] books

2. The best way to search for information in the library is to...

   [A] browse among the shelves
   [B] ask a friend
   [C] use the library catalogue, OPAC

Final hints and tips for development

The main thing to remember is that you need to communicate your content using the simplest terms possible. Try to avoid jargon. I know this is hard in the library context, but you must keep your language plain and simple, especially if you are training people whose first language is not English. For terms like OPAC which we cannot do without, explain why the word is used; that it's an acronym for the term online public access catalogue. After all, it is quicker and easier to say 'OPAC' than it is to say 'library catalogue'.

Wilder and Rotondo (2002) urge trainers to ensure their content is of interest to the trainees; to do this, you often have to customise your sessions. In addition to this, as each class could be different, you may find yourself having to modify your sessions as what works for one group may totally fail to interest the next group. All your search demonstrations, for example, should use keywords that are directly related to each group's assignments. It is better to find out before the workshop what these assignments are so that you can test your searches. I find that if I ask the trainees for examples during the session, they either cannot think of anything or they choose something that I cannot think of synonyms for at the time, and the database fails to yield any hits.

Closely related to customisation, is the provision of a backup plan. Always have backups of any presentations in more than one format because, according to Murphy's Law, if you save your work onto a portable 'pen drive', the trainer's computer will have a damaged USB connection. I find that what usually works for me is loading my presentations onto the library server and then having a backup copy on CD. I also check the trainer's PC before the training to see if the CD drive is still working. You also need a backup plan for emergencies, as my colleague discovered when he went to a tiny island in Micronesia:

My friend and I were teaching a course on Internet searching skills. This was a hands-on course and midway through the class there was a power outage. We immediately started to panic, especially after having come from a country where there is an uninterrupted power supply and companies are fined for power outages. The technical help informed us that he did not know when the power would return. My quick-thinking friend decided we move the class onto the veranda. He threw me the challenge of then continuing the class.

We were teaching search engines and how spiders work. Taking the class outside allowed us to do an activity that demonstrated how search engines crawled the Web. The class loved it and actually found spiders and their webs on the veranda. Lady Luck was on our side and within an hour or so, we had power. Phew! Some participants even reflected this in their feedback form – that the outdoor activity was the best part of the programme. (Rajendra Munoo – librarian, Singapore)

When developing your course, as part of your preparation for the training, always have a little pool of training games and alternatives to fall back on in case something goes wrong. Even if you have to give a lecture as opposed to a hands-on workshop, be it due to emergencies or other constraints, there are plenty of things you can do to engage your trainees and allow them to have fun. Apart from the example above, an activity to do with searching databases that doesn't use technology could involve getting the trainees to think of synonyms for selected words. You could even make it a race to see who can think of the most synonyms within a certain time limit. Just remember to make the whole learning experience fun.

5

Implementation: deliver the goods

- Presentation *methods*.
- Prepare the *room*.
- Prepare *yourself*.
- *Test* everything twice.

The implementation stage of the ADDIE model of instructional design is probably the most difficult part, especially for those who dread the thought of having to stand up and talk in front of a whole lot of people. This stage also requires the most work on your part, as you constantly have to watch what you are saying and monitor how the trainees are receiving your words of wisdom. 'Know yourself and develop your own style' is some excellent advice offered by a colleague of mine. Her suggestion:

> Don't try too hard to be someone else. Make your style work for you and the learners. It is when you are comfortable that your learners feel comfortable with you. (Eng Mui Hong – manager, learning and development, Singapore)

You may have watched an admired colleague in a training situation and wanted to be able to take the same approach, or you may have felt that the way you were training was not quite right. I am not entirely sure that there can be a definite right or wrong way of training, as each of us should be training according to our own style. The most important thing is that your trainees should be absorbing what you want them to absorb, so you need to make sure that you don't get too bogged down with what you yourself are doing. The same colleague talks of 'Less of you, More of them':

> ...focus on the learning climate and how the learners are learning rather than on how you, as a trainer or facilitator, are doing. Overemphasis on the latter tends to make you very self-conscious and leaves little energy for you to consider how to be responsive to the learners' needs. (Eng Mui Hong – manager, learning and development, Singapore)

Eye contact

When it comes to the learners' needs, if you are well prepared your content will cater for these needs, but you also need to watch how the learners receive your delivery of this content. All good trainers are able to respond immediately to any mood changes or wandering of attention during a workshop and they do this by keeping a constant watch on the trainees. If you are constantly making eye contact with your trainees, you will be able to watch their facial expressions and so gauge their reactions during the training.

You can see the students getting bored, for example, when they start e-mailing or even chatting to their friends. Don't try to speed up your presentation to get it over with, rather try to increase their involvement by throwing in a pop quiz or giving them an impromptu task. If the noise level within the training room starts rising so that others have difficulty hearing what you are saying, don't try to talk louder or you could find yourself yelling in an effort to make yourself heard. I have found that to stand silently in front of the class is far more effective. The other trainees will get the noise makers to be quiet for you.

Noise is not always such a bad thing either as it could mean that the trainees are having great fun during a planned activity. While some trainers see too much noise as being indicative of a loss of control, sometimes it doesn't help to be too rigid in your approach. Be assertive and not autocratic. After all, your aim is not to stifle the trainees but to give them the opportunity to learn.

Getting a response

On the opposite end of the scale, there are times when you will not be able to get the trainees to respond, no matter how hard you try. Many people are initially reluctant to begin interacting in a class. They worry that they may have the wrong answer, or they are afraid of appearing foolish. The first thing to remember in such a situation is not to be afraid of silence. Many of us tend to quickly ask another question instead of giving the trainees enough time to formulate an answer. Try the nursery rhyme trick where you say the rhyme quietly in your head (for about 20 seconds) to stop yourself from trying to break the silence too soon. The second thing to remember is that you must have the question written down somewhere, on a whiteboard or on one of your presentation slides. The trainees can then read and re-read the question for themselves and so minimise any possible misunderstandings caused by different pronunciations, for example.

The third thing to remember is not to start with the difficult stuff. Always begin with simple questions that are easy to answer, so the trainees don't feel too threatened. Speaking up in class can be just as frightening for the trainees, as training is for some of us. Jolles (2002) has some very useful ideas here and, like a trainer in a recent course that I attended, his philosophy is that there are 'no dumb questions'. In other words, we should always respect every question that is asked, thank the trainee who is doing the asking and do our best to provide an answer. Of course, in some cases we will not know the answer, but it is perfectly acceptable to promise to get back to the trainee at a later stage. Just make a note of the question and find the answer for the trainee after the workshop.

Questions

Jolles (2002) also has suggestions for the types of questions we can ask, as well as the way in which we can ask them. One simple question to start with could involve trainee opinion. The answers in this case are not as important as the overall aim of reducing anxiety. Another type of question is the problem-based one where we ask the trainees for a solution to a scenario. Here we need to give the trainees a much longer time to find the answer, it would also be preferable to allow them to work in groups too. When it comes to the way in which we ask these questions, one rule of thumb is that nearly all of the questions should be open ended, without yes or no answers being possible. This method might be harder than you think, but gets easier with a little effort and lots of practice.

Jolles (2002) provides four different techniques for asking questions:

- *Guided technique.* These are the questions that we ask of specific trainees. We need to ensure that these questions are as non-threatening as possible as we could be putting the trainees on the spot here.

- *Overhead technique.* The most common technique, these are the general questions thrown open to the group where anyone can provide the answer.

- *Relay technique.* Here we are looking for an answer to the same question from each trainee. These would usually be the 'yes/no' type of question like whether or not the trainees have attended a previous course. Asking trainees what they learned in a prior session, for example, will come up with the same answers, so the last trainees to answer will usually end up agreeing with what has already been said.

- *Reverse technique.* This is where, when a trainee asks a question, you ask the rest of the trainees for the answer. Be careful of the technique, however, as it can get extremely irritating. One trainer I know used this technique to answer nearly all the questions asked and ended up having to explain to a group of very annoyed adult trainees why she was doing this.

Whatever the question, our job as trainers is to make it safe for the trainees to answer. Be encouraging and respectful. Never use sarcasm, even with the most irritating trainee and try not to single anyone out. If you notice someone is particularly shy, don't try to force participation out of them. You will always find people who will not want to get involved, no matter how hard you try, and it helps if you respect this sometimes.

The trainees may also have their own questions. Try to give them the opportunity to ask them throughout the session by pausing for a while after you have introduced an important concept. Asking for questions at the end doesn't usually work, as students, in particular, just want to get to their next lesson. If you have a longer training session, questions are usually asked during the tea and lunch breaks. Once back in the workshop, you could repeat the question for the rest of the class and provide the answer again. If you only have a few hours, however, call for questions periodically during the session. In my experience, I get more questions if I move around the room during the group activities. This gets me closer to the trainees and gives the shyer people more of a chance to speak to me. After I have answered such a question, I then share it with the rest of the trainees.

You will also get those questions that have nothing to do with the topic in hand. Try to minimise these by making your objectives very clear from the start. If you can remind the class of these objectives, it is then easier for you to gently dismiss the question as not being part of the scope of your lesson. If you think it is important, you can always tell the trainee that you would be willing to discuss the answer after the session. In the little scene I described in Chapter 1, where the participants kept on asking me to clarify cataloguing rules, I had glossed over the objectives because I thought there wasn't enough time. As it turns out, I could have saved much more time if the trainees were given a better idea of what to expect from me.

Maintaining interest

When it comes to keeping the trainees interested, Jolles (2002) has 20 tips for us. He recommends that we use:

- *Tone of voice.* Wallace (2001), as mentioned in Chapter 4, also stresses the importance of varying the tone of your voice. There is nothing like a description of library databases, delivered in a monotone, for putting people to sleep!

- *Stories and jokes.* If you interpret the information and illustrate it with jokes and stories, it becomes easier to understand and remember. Real-life stories and examples are preferable, as people tend to remember them better. One of my favourite stories to break up the monotony of a list of interview techniques for business students, is the one about testing. Many years ago I applied for a job as a trainee store manager in the retail world and the interviewer made me take one of those aptitude tests. Apparently my marks were among the highest he had ever seen and I consequently got the job. I was, of course, totally unsuited to the job, so taking the test turned out to be a waste of everyone's time – indeed, I am still not sure what I was being tested for. The point of this story is to show the students that they need to evaluate the information that they find. One source of information may recommend the use of an aptitude test, but another source may suggest these tests are worthless as an interview tool.

- *Movement.* Moving around the room while you present your material conveys the impression that you are comfortable with your subject and you know what you are talking about. Just think of those trainers who sit behind a desk for the whole session – you can just see how nervous they are. Be aware, however, of how you are moving. I once watched a presenter take one step forward and then one step back for the entire session. At one stage I found myself considering the use of superglue on the sole of his shoe! Movement also introduces a change of pace in that you can get the trainees to move around to form groups, but remember that this will be time-consuming, so factor the extra time into your lesson plan.

- *Change of pace.* Always vary the pace of your training to keep up the interest levels, but watch your time and don't spend too long or too short a time on any one section. If problems arise, promise to get back to the trainees via e-mail, for example.

- *Handouts.* Handouts can be used to entertain the trainees while you are waiting for everyone to arrive for a session. They can also be used as a change of pace during the training and to flesh out concepts that are only touched upon. Keep the language used in the handouts simple, with lots of tables, illustrations, white space and not too much text. Use headings and bulleted lists to emphasise important points.

- *Trainee names.* This is a difficult one as many of us as librarians get to train students only once or twice in very short sessions. Getting to know names under these circumstances is nearly impossible and sometimes our task is made even harder.

> I was working in an Arab country once and teaching a course on research skills. As most of the girls had their faces covered, it was really difficult trying to know their names and who was who. I made it a point to associate and identify the girls by the handbags they carried. (Rajendra Munoo – librarian, Singapore)

Of course, like women everywhere, these girls would change their handbags and the first indication my colleague would get of his using the wrong names would be the sound of smothered giggles. You could overcome this type of situation by getting the trainees to wear name tags, but they would need to be large enough for you to read them swiftly. Hesitating over a name will just highlight what you don't know.

- *Visual aids.* Visual aids are always useful, especially if you are a beginner trainer, as they can enhance learning as well as help to remind you of what to say.

- *Questions.* Adding to what I said previously in this chapter, try to spread the question asking over the entire session and don't always ask the same type of questions.

- *Group activities.* Group activities are very useful as a change of pace, as well as a form of active learning.

- *Personalisation.* This is in keeping with my colleague, Eng Mui Hong's recommendation of knowing yourself and developing your own style. Little signs of personalisation show that you have made an effort with your presentation and that you are comfortable with the topic. Involving your trainees also works well. I once included a book review by a student. I extracted a paragraph from this review and asked the class to tell me who wrote it. As they were expecting some well-known author to have written it, they were delighted to find out that it was actually the work of one of their own.

- *Humour.* Bringing a little laughter to a session makes the trainees feel more comfortable, but don't go overboard. Learning should be fun, but learning still needs to take place.

- *Non-verbal communication.* You need to be aware of the message you are sending out with your non-verbal behaviour. Some signs of nervousness are acceptable, but others will just become annoying; for example, I used to fiddle with an elastic band. I used to pull on it and stretch it and then drop it and have to pick it up all the time. I didn't even realise how this must have looked until I read Jolles' book!

- *Differing techniques.* If you are planning to cater for the different learning styles, you will have already included different ways of getting your message across. Aim for a well balanced mixture of lecturing, discussion, group activity and so on.

- *Co-presenters.* Another way to vary your pace and technique is to get someone to help you present. This is especially useful if you are really nervous about training. For example, each of you could present the section of the session that you are most familiar with. Alternatively, your co-presenter could help with trainee questions, group activity facilitation and crowd control. Even if the lecturers concerned attend the workshop with their students, don't rely on them for help, as they may keep quiet to avoid interfering.

  Allan (2003) warns us to follow certain basic rules when using co-presenters. If we are to train with another person, we need to be sure that they have the same ideas about training that we do. For example, you cannot have your co-presenter sniffing disapprovingly at your methods during the session. You and your co-presenters should also discuss before the sessions how you will introduce each other, what the person not training is expected to do, what will happen if one of you makes a mistake and needs to be corrected and so on. Make sure you both know what you have to do and when and how you will be doing it.

  You could also use facilitators in your training sessions. These people don't do any of the actual training, but can be extremely useful in keeping the trainees on track and for answering questions during the group activities. If you are nervous about training and have to present to large groups, facilitators can be invaluable. The facilitators are also the people who can see which parts of your presentation are unclear to the trainees. Feedback from facilitators and co-trainers can help you fine-tune your lesson plan as well as your delivery.

- *Competition.* A little competition can be great fun. For example, you could see who gets to be the first person to come up with three synonyms for a certain keyword. The reward for the winner could be praise, or a small candy. The good news for those of us with a zero budget for prizes is that candies and the like should not be used too often, as the emphasis should be on the answer and not on the prize. At times I have used only the 'thought' of a candy, that is, I tell the winners that if I had a chocolate, it would have been theirs. If the praise is sincere, the trainees don't seem to mind the lack of edible treats too much.

- *Something different.* If you are confident enough, you can try something unusual, like asking the trainees to identify an obscure song. If you don't specify that they search the Web using the song lyrics as keywords, it takes them a while to think of it. This is a good way of pointing out that research happens all the time in our everyday lives.

- *Deviations.* Some straying from the topic can be a good way of encouraging discussion and learning, but don't stray too far from your original objectives. Watch the trainees not directly involved in the discussion for signs of boredom, as this will show that it is time to get back to the lesson plan.

- *Music.* Music can be a useful way to create certain moods, but you will need to select the correct kind as people's tastes vary. In addition, I wouldn't advocate the use of music during the actual training. Most trainers I know who do use music, switch it off to indicate they are ready to begin training.

- *Breaks.* The longer workshops, like those that last more than three hours, will need to have some sort of break provided for the trainees. If you are going to provide breaks, don't expect to do so at exactly the same time in every session. You need to keep an eye on your trainees and, as far as possible, try to stop when they need a break. You will have a carefully prepared lesson plan, but you must be ready to improvise or, as a more experienced trainer, scrap the plan altogether.

- *Enthusiasm.* With a subject that many people see as boring, it is especially important for librarians as trainers to show enthusiasm. We can hardly expect our trainees to get excited about the topic if we ourselves are not.

Presentation skills

Sherman (2002) says that there are ten things we can do when we are presenting to make our sessions really remarkable:

- *Have a strong beginning.* Many trainers start off by introducing themselves and the course and then they dive straight into the content. Some of us even apologise for not feeling well. Neither approach is going to excite our trainees or make them sit up and pay attention and professing to feeling ill makes the trainees wonder what we would have been like if we had been on top form. Sherman tells us to 'start with a bang', or use a powerful attention grabber. Our introduction can also be used as the icebreaker. If you can find an interesting story in the newspaper, then use that. You could also use a funny personal experience, a quote, a cartoon, or even a startling bit of trivia; just make sure that what you use can be related to your training in some way.

Some authors recommend that you establish your credibility as a trainer before you begin the session, but I am not convinced that the students need to hear this right away. Given that we work in a library, it goes without saying that we should know at least something about using the library facilities. If you feel it necessary, you could mention during the session your years of experience or something similar, but my feeling is that your credibility will become more apparent with the knowledge you demonstrate of your topic.

- *Use your own speaking style.* As I have said before, you must use your own training style. If you are comfortable, then you can relax and help your trainees learn. If, like me, you have a soft voice, make sure you speak loudly enough for the trainees to hear, or use a microphone and ask your trainees to signal you if your voice starts to soften during the session. You also need to remember to speak clearly, avoid slang and repeat your main points. Don't try to be cool by using teenage jargon when training these young adults; the longer it has been since you were a teenager, the sillier you could end up looking.

- *'Work the room'.* Sherman's advice to 'work the room' is not something that I agree with in the library context, as I prefer Jolles' (2001) way of thinking. Sherman says we should arrive early and speak to the trainees in order to find out more about them. Jolles, however, states that we should leave the trainees to their own devices before the session; his reasoning being that he wants the trainees to settle down and get comfortable on their own. Jolles also feels that it is better to answer questions in front of the whole group so that everyone gets the chance to learn. I have found that it works better for me to leave the trainees on their own with some handouts and greet everyone at the door as they enter. Of course, you do have to 'work the room' during the training. Make eye contact for at least three seconds at a time and keep a close watch on how your trainees are receiving content.

- *Relax.* This would probably be the most difficult advice for most of us to follow and Sherman recommends techniques like deep breathing or listening to soothing music. I would suggest that you also just accept that you are going to be nervous and prepare yourself and your materials as well as you possibly can. The knowledge that you have a well-designed plan always minimises the fear, so preparation could be used as the solution to any anxiety problem.

- *Don't read, speak.* Do not read off your slides or your notes; this is never well received as it is merely boring and makes you look like you don't know your topic. Instead, use bulleted points on your slides and elaborate from there.

- *Use personal stories.* I have found that talking about my personal experiences over the years helps to gain attention and make it easier for the trainees to remember certain points. I would imagine this is because people are always interested in what happens to others – just look at the popularity of 'reality television'.

- *Speak from the heart.* My colleague from South Africa agrees wholeheartedly with this sentiment:

The most important advice I would give to would-be trainers is: speak from the heart. It's the most significant advice I ever received. Despite the fact that we are encouraged to look at the message and not the messenger, that's what people will do. When we speak from our hearts we are real, sincere and therefore believable. It's what people will respond to, and they will forgive any number of mistakes from someone who is warm, friendly, kind and generous with their time and energy. (Susie Spies – environmental education trainer, South Africa)

- *Have a strong ending.* The first lesson plan that I ever saw used a question and answer session to end off the training and it really puzzled me that, no matter how many times I asked, I never received any questions. All the trainees were in too much of a hurry to leave and I always ended up feeling as though the session was not finished. It is far better to end with a summary of the objectives and a quote that ties in with the topic or with campus life, for example. You also need to know when to stop talking so the trainees know that you have definitely reached the end. Sometimes we are tempted to clarify something again, even after we have said goodbye. This usually results in us yelling over the heads of the trainees who are leaving the room – not a satisfying ending at all.

- *Prepare well.* In the first chapter I provided a quote by Alexander Graham Bell and, as I cannot stress enough the importance of preparation, I will give you the quote again:

Before anything else, preparation is the key to success.

Meticulous preparation not only ensures the successful delivery of your training session, it also helps to lessen those feelings of anxiety. If you know you are well prepared and you have all your backup plans in place, you can be ready for anything.

■ *Recognise that speaking is an acquired skill.* The anxiety levels in our library always increase exponentially as the annual departmental meeting draws nearer. This is because our boss often selects people from outside of the management sphere to give presentations. She does this as part of a people development programme, building on the awareness that public speaking does not come naturally and so giving all of us the chance to practise. By the time the staff have delivered a couple of presentations, it is obvious that the thought of the delivery no longer gives them sleepless nights. In the same way, you will find that training will get easier and easier the more sessions you deliver, because practice can make perfect.

Prepare the room

The first thing you need to do when preparing the training room is to make sure that it is adequately signposted. I once attended a course where we were given the address of the building and the number of the room. When we arrived, there was no one at the reception desk and no signs posted anywhere. We were expected to make our way to the room on the second floor of the building, but none of the numerous e-mails we each received made this clear to us. As a result of this unsettling experience, many of us started having doubts about the quality of the session we were about to attend.

It may strike you as unfair, but the venue and its location do have an impact on your training. Your venue must be easy to find, or you need to provide explicit instructions. Do not assume that if the trainees have attended one of your courses before, they will know where to find you the next time, and ensure that coordinating lecturing staff also have detailed instructions. Don't rely on other people to pass the word; you need to inform everyone yourself.

You can also spruce up the appearance of a dull training room by putting up posters on the walls, using what your library receives from your local library association, for example. Sometimes library training rooms are also used as storage areas for extra chairs and it might help to cover the resulting mess with a colourful cloth. Allan (2003) even advocates the use of a vase of flowers and aromatherapy oils in the room. Most of the time we don't have much choice as to the layout of the room, the number of computers and chairs, lighting, the position of the trainer's computer and so on, but we can introduce these little extra touches to show that we have made the effort.

You also need to make the effort to be at the training room before your trainees. Apart from being early so you can prepare the room, it is always a good thing to greet your trainees at the door with a welcoming smile. Give them handouts to keep them occupied, have background music playing and leave them to their own devices before you start the session itself.

The equipment

When it comes to equipment and facilities that could break down or stop working, unless you are able to deal with it yourself, always ensure that you know who is available for support and how you can get hold of these people. While it would be preferable to manage this aspect of training for yourself (after all, it is faster than having to call someone else in), not all of us are so technologically inclined. Regardless of whether or not you need the help of others, it helps to build up a good relationship with these support staff, as they are the ones you will need to call upon in times of crisis.

Even if you are not going to be doing your own trouble shooting, if you are using a computer, you will need to have at least a basic idea of how it works. Find out which power and connector cables the equipment uses, for example, so if one of the cables gets accidently pulled out if people walk over it, you can at least reconnect it. Disable any computer screensavers, set up a short-cut on the computer desktop to your presentation, and have a mouse connected to those laptops with the fiddly touch pads. The last thing you want to do is fumble around with unfamiliar navigation controls in front of a class. Remember too that laptop keyboards differ, so if you are going to be using a laptop, find out where all the keys that you will need are situated.

When you are checking to see if the colours you have used in your presentation show up well on the projection screen, find out which light switches control which lights. If you have a choice, switch off the lights that shine onto the screen. Of course, not everyone will have such a choice, so you could switch off all the lights and speak in a darkened room – not an ideal situation, as you or any writing materials may be hard to see. You can also try to use colours that stand up better to harsh lights, for example, black text on a plain white background. I once had to use an elderly projector that made the screen look as if it was going mouldy down the right hand side. I simply changed the background colour of my slides to match the mould so it was no longer noticeable.

You also need to look at the more mundane matters like who is in charge of keeping the room and facilities clean and tidy. At my institution, the cleaners come in when the room first gets opened for the day, so I know I need to open early enough for them to do their thing. After each session then, it is my responsibility to switch off the computers and lights, return the chairs to their original positions and just generally put the room back in order. Minor but important details such as these also include the replenishment of refreshments, if you are going to provide them, when you can start using the room, when you have to be out, and who holds the keys. I received a frantic call one Saturday morning from a staff member on campus who was given the wrong key. She had prepared the training venue the day before, when the room had been open, but she couldn't gain access on the day of the actual training. As the library was the only department open on Saturday, she was phoning to see if she could use our venue. Such last minute scrambles can be very stressful for a trainer, so we should do everything we possibly can to avoid them.

One final word about the training equipment involves what Allan (2003) refers to as the trainer's kit, that is, those things that you should never be without when you are training. Have a large bag or briefcase that all your handouts will fit into, with room to spare and make sure you have the following:

- pens and pencils;
- extra paper;
- whiteboard markers;
- a backup presentation on disk or CD and on pen drive;
- electrical adaptor;
- portable music player with batteries, in case there is no suitable player on the computer;
- two or three different styles of music CDs;

- free gifts or candy, if you use these as bribes and rewards;
- water;
- tissues (for the whiteboard as well as your nose); and
- throat lozenges.

Prepare yourself

You have prepared your lesson plan so you know what to train, the trainees know when and where the training will be held, and the room and facilities are ready and waiting. Now all you have left to do is to prepare yourself.

> One of my most embarrassing moments happened in the middle of winter. I have one pair of black and one pair of navy pumps. That morning, in the dark, I grabbed shoes and it was only at tea time when I realised some participants were looking at my feet and chuckling. I looked down and yes, I was wearing mismatched shoes. What could I do? I laughed with them and told them how silly I felt and it was over. (Susie Spies – environmental education trainer, Singapore)

You need to pay careful attention to how you dress when you deliver your training. The general advice is to dress one level up from your trainees so that you look professional but not unapproachable. If I am going to be training students, I wear dress trousers and a shirt, for example, whereas if I have to train academic staff, I usually end up wearing a suit. A lot will depend on the dress codes of your particular institution.

Whatever you decide to wear, make sure you are comfortable wearing clothes that are neither too tight nor too loose and that your underwear does not show through or peek out. Your favourite black thong may be really comfortable, but if it keeps on appearing at your trouser waistband when you sit down, your trainees will not be paying much attention to what you are saying. Check all your zipper and button fastenings, as well as your hemlines, as you need to present a tidy appearance, and don't wear dangling or clanking jewellery. You want the trainees to pay attention to your words, not what you are wearing.

It isn't just your clothes that matter; you need to watch your attitude. Show that you care about how much your trainees learn. Project warmth and enthusiasm, listen to what they have to say, smile and give genuine compliments. Train from the heart, but be assertive when it is necessary. Sometimes, a discussion will take you away from the training objectives and you will need to bring the class firmly back into focus. Above all, don't take anything personally. If a few trainees insist on constantly sending text messages to their friends' mobile phones, it does not mean that you are a bad trainer so don't get disheartened. Either ask them to stop or, if they are not causing any disturbance, let them carry on. You have your other trainees to look after.

Test everything twice

Before you even think of starting your training, you must have tested everything twice on more than one computer, and not just the first part of your presentation either. This is very important; something which a colleague of mine discovered the hard way. She had created a lively PowerPoint slide show with animation, sound effects and music to entertain a class of freshmen during orientation. She tested the show twice before the actual day and found everything to be in working order. Sadly, sometimes the sound on a PowerPoint slide will not play when you move the presentation to another computer and this is just what happened to her. Halfway through the slides, the sound disappeared and the technicians could not get it started up again before the end of the show. As a result, these first year students missed out on some important information about the library. So don't forget your testing.

6

Evaluation: decide if it really worked

- Different *techniques* and *types*.
- *Survey* for reactions.
- *Analysing* the results.

When it comes to training, your work does not end when the last trainee walks out of the door. You may be tempted at this stage to sit back and heave a huge sigh of relief, but you still have a lot more to do before you can start patting yourself on the back. This is the time when you have to decide whether or not you were successful in meeting your objectives. You can do this by using a number of different evaluation, assessment or testing techniques. Various researchers have used these three terms interchangeably, as they have very similar definitions, but I tend to favour the term 'evaluation' as it is the one used by the ADDIE model, while I will use 'test' to refer to a tool for the evaluation.

In addition to the evaluation techniques, you also have a number of different areas to examine, however, and you need to do this before your formulate your evaluation programme. According to Lindauer (2004), these areas would include:

- *The learning environment.* You need to look at how your training programme ties in with what is happening in the rest of your institution. Working in isolation often leads to a duplication of effort, as you may find yourself repeating elements of a programme from another department on your campus. You might also have to comply with a wider set of directives than just those set by the library.

- *Information literacy programme components.* Decide whether or not your training session relates in some way to other information literacy programme efforts, if any, on the part of the library. Perhaps you could deliver your sessions as an extension of an already existing programme. Do not forget to use the findings generated by other and/or previous programmes so you don't repeat the mistakes made by others.

- *Student learning outcomes.* Involved here are the different evaluation techniques. See if you can make use of the analysis of scores and feedback from any previous assessments that have been conducted. You may even be able to insert one or two of your own questions into a colleague's evaluation questionnaire, rather than having a separate one.

Different techniques

The most commonly used techniques for evaluation consist of:

- *Surveys.* To give you an idea of trainee attitudes and emotional responses.

- *Tests.* These can be conducted before, or before and after the programme in the form of multiple choice quizzes or short essays to gauge how much the trainees have learned.

- *Assignments.* These can be set, either by the academic staff concerned or the librarian, and can involve the finding of a specified number of books and journal articles on a topic, for example.

- *Research records.* Some lecturers require their students to keep records of their research activities in the form of journals or diaries.

- *Student grades.* You could ask the lecturers to provide you with the marks the students get for their subject during the course of the year.

- *Bibliography analysis.* This would be one of the most difficult and time-consuming techniques as you would need to peruse each bibliography and rate it according to certain pre-set criteria. For example, you could check whether the bibliography adheres to the preferred citation style rules, or if there is evidence of research beyond merely finding books from the library catalogue. Middleton (2005) conducted a study on the analysis of student bibliographies and came up with some very interesting findings as to what has an impact on the quality of these bibliographies. If you plan to use this evaluation technique, the methods used by Middleton would be most helpful for your planning.

When you are trying to decide which evaluation techniques to use, I would suggest that you do three things:

- *Look at what others have done.* Look at how other librarians and educators have approached their own evaluation programmes. You could perhaps start with the programmes reviewed in Chapter 4. The TIP programme from the University of Wyoming Libraries, for example, makes use of a very comprehensive set of questions.

- *Look at existing guidelines and standards.* Look at the guidelines and standards that have been put in place by the Association of College and Research Libraries (ACRL). Most librarians find the ACRL recommendations extremely useful. Their website can be found at *http://www.ala.org/ala/acrl/acrlstandards/standardsguidelines.htm.* Williams (2000) takes an in-depth look at evaluation, providing examples of question types and pointing to the Educational Testing Service (ETS) online. While her link to the ETS is now out of date, if you go to the website at *http://www.etx.org/testcoll/* you will be able to search the test collection that she describes.

- *Ask yourself all those why, what, how and who questions.* In order to help you gauge whether or not your programme has resulted in any trainee learning or changes in their research behaviour, ask yourself a number of questions. As suggested by Allan (2003), these questions include asking yourself:

  – Why

    • Why are you going to assess your training?

  – What

    • What are the objectives that are going to be met?

    • What information will you be looking for?

    • What criteria will be used for marking?

    • What resources do you have access to?

    • What will happen to the results?

  – How

    • How will you carry out the evaluation?

    • How will you gather the information?

– Who

- Who will be doing all the work?
- Who will report on or present the findings?
- Who will be using these findings?

Different types

The type of test that you eventually decide to use will depend on a number of different factors, the most important of which being your training objectives and your reasons for testing. Sometimes the results of the test are not as important as the feedback you will be receiving; indeed, perhaps you developed your test to serve as a revision exercise only. Just remember to keep the following in mind when creating the actual test:

- Some people, especially adult learners, don't like idea of a test as it brings back too many stressful school memories. Stolovitch and Keeps (2003) suggest that instead of using the word 'test', you prefer words or phrases like 'practice' and 'check yourself'.

- Test only your objectives.

- Provide very clear instructions, as well as details for whom to contact when help is needed.

- To put the trainees at ease, begin with easy questions which gradually get harder and harder. This will be a problem, however, if you are going to randomise your question order. Sometimes, in an effort to encourage the students to think about their answers instead of copying, librarians make the test questions appear in a different order every time the test is accessed – an easy thing to do if you are using Blackboard. You may decide that randomisation is more important than trying to put the trainees at ease – it will depend on how you use test grades.

■ Avoid all ambiguity, especially when it comes to the answers.

■ Keep your language simple.

■ Trainees are more likely to complete a test (or survey, for that matter) if you catch them before they leave the training room. Asking them to complete tests later usually takes a lot of effort and reminding on your part.

Stolovitch and Keeps (2003) provide a very useful table of different test types and include the pros and cons involved with each type. These types include:

■ True/false or yes/no – trainee selects one answer from two options.

  – Pros

    ● Most people are familiar with this type of question.

    ● It is quick and easy to formulate the questions and the instructions.

    ● They are simple to create with JavaScript.

    ● They form part of the available options in learning management systems like BlackBoard and WebCT.

    ● They are easy to mark.

  – Cons

    ● You need to know your subject very well.

    ● Trainees can select the answers without much thought and still have a 50/50 chance of getting them right.

- Multiple choice – trainee selects one or more answers from a number of options.
  - Pros
    - Most people are familiar with this type of question.
    - It is easy to formulate the instructions.
    - They are simple to create with JavaScript.
    - They form part of the available options in learning management systems like BlackBoard and WebCT.
    - They are easy to mark.
  - Cons
    - Careful thought is needed to develop good questions that do not confuse and yet still test learning.
    - Trainees can learn to guess the answers.
- Drag and drop or matching – trainee selects an available answer to match a question.
  - Pros
    - Can be easy to create the questions.
    - They form part of the available options in learning management systems like BlackBoard and WebCT.
    - They are easy to mark.
    - They can be great fun for the trainees to complete.
  - Cons
    - The more interesting versions require a knowledge of Flash.
    - Trainees can guess the answers.
- Short answer – trainees complete a sentence or answer a question with a few words or short essay.
  - Pros
    - Can be easy to create the questions.

- They form part of the available options in learning management systems like BlackBoard and WebCT.
- Can generate very useful feedback.
- Cons
  - These are much harder to mark.
  - Can place too much pressure on the trainees who will already have been given large assignment loads from their lecturers.

Survey for reactions

Usually the tests at the end of a training session are for summative evaluation purposes. In other words, what you want to know is the effect that your training has had. Did they enjoy the session? Did they learn anything? Is their research behaviour likely to change as a result of what they have learned? During the training, however, you should have been collecting feedback for what is known as formative evaluation. This involves constantly watching for the reaction of the trainees to the content and delivery of your training. If one of your jokes fell flat, are you able to figure why the trainees did not respond? If you cannot find a reason, perhaps you should scrap the joke altogether and try another one.

Just remember that formative evaluation is liable to be extremely subjective. What works well with one group may spell disaster with the second group, but it helps to get a general idea of how your delivery is received. Surveys for generic evaluation, that is, comments from the trainees, can also be prone to subjectivity and sometimes are not at all useful. I have had comments that included requests for food to be provided, more computers to be bought and the training to be held at an earlier time slot, for example. What with budget restrictions and being allocated specific time slots by the lecturers, there was not much I could do about responses like these.

One way to minimise comments that you cannot act upon, is to be very specific about what type of comments you require. Instead of asking 'How can we improve this session?' rather ask something like 'If you felt that this session was too long, please tell us why you thought so'. Of course, getting so specific involves asking many more questions, which may annoy the trainees. You just need to find a balance that suits your purposes.

Analysis of the results

Ondrusek et al. (2005) describe the creation and implementation of an information literacy testing tool at the Hunter College in New York. The librarians at the college began their evaluation with 42 test questions, but by the fourth run, they had trimmed it down to 32 randomised questions. They used a mixture of different test types – true/false, multiple choice, matching and short answer – and they provide us with examples of these tests, as well as detailed information on how they used Microsoft Excel to analyse the results.

How you analyse the results of your evaluation will depend on how you are going to be using them. You may be carrying out the evaluation merely to improve upon your training techniques, to show the lecturers concerned how much their students have been able to learn, or you may have to justify the existence of your training programme to your institution's management. One of the main reasons that I carry out evaluations of my training programmes is that

I always find it interesting to see how I have done. Just remember – some of the comments are not meant to be taken personally. Even if the analysis is meant only for you, you need to ensure that others can understand it, as the past programme evaluations of others can be invaluable when designing your own new programmes.

7

Conclusion

I was teaching a class in a less developed country and was making use of some overhead transparencies. I had projected a transparency onto the wall and went forward to teach from it. After completing the first concept, I was supposed to reveal the second concept. I began to push up on the wall thinking I was moving the transparency higher. After three attempts I realised my folly, but by then the class were rolling in laughter. (Rajendra Munoo – librarian, Singapore)

Training can be exhausting, nerve-wracking, or even, as the story above so graphically illustrates, downright embarrassing. To stand in front of a whole lot of people and try to get them interested in a subject like library research skills which, let's face it, can be incredibly boring, is not everybody's cup of tea. I firmly believe, however, that if your training sessions end up putting your trainees to sleep, it is because you are not trying hard enough.

Your efforts also need to be directed at ensuring that everyone involved in the training agrees that library workshops are being taught to improve the trainees' library research skills.

Effective training should result in improved performance and this can only happen when trainees and staff

> approach it from this perspective. (Madi McAllister –
> workforce development advisor, London, UK)

I have had lecturers approach me with requests for online library tutorials because they have been instructed by their departmental heads to place a certain percentage of their courses online. If they use an online library tutorial, these lecturers are then able to fulfil their own online requirements. This does not, I am afraid, result in very high class participation rates, as the students end up seeing the tutorial as something that can be skipped if they run out of time.

So it is that, as library staff, we often start our library user education at a distinct disadvantage. First, our trainees are hardly ever wildly excited about attending library workshops – most of them seem to be labouring under the misapprehension that, as everything is now available on the Web, there is no need for a comprehensive library research skills course. Second, academic staff often do not see the need for library workshops either.

It is up to us, therefore, to provide (and market) training programmes that are seen by both the trainees and their lecturers as being useful as well as enjoyable, and the ADDIE model of instructional systems design can help us do just this. While there are a number of different interpretations of this model, each version makes use of the same five basic stages:

- *Analysis* – thinking about the trainees.
- *Design* – considering the objectives.
- *Development* – creating the course.
- *Implementation* – delivering the goods.
- *Evaluation* – deciding if it really worked.

With the analysis stage, we concentrate on our trainees. We look at who they are, what their expectations are and what they need from library research skills training, with the different learning styles and learning theories playing an important part. Above all, we strive to answer their question of what's in it for them. In the design stage, we consider our training objectives. The more time and effort we expend on these objectives, the easier it will be for us to develop the rest of the programme. We also need to consider a few more theories about how people learn.

During the development stage, we get down to the actual creation of the course itself. It is always helpful to look at what other librarians and educators have already accomplished, as we may be able, with the existence of an open publication licence, to adapt an existing programme for our own needs. TILT from the Texas System Digital Library and TIP from the University of Wyoming Libraries are two such tutorials that are being used by libraries other than those that developed the programmes.

The implementation stage involves the setting up of the training room, the thorough testing of the presentation and personal preparation. How we deliver the training makes a vast difference to how it will be received, but we need to find a delivery style that makes us comfortable while enabling learning on the part of the trainees. And finally, in the evaluation stage, we need to decide if we have been effective in meeting our training objectives. If we have managed to meet our objectives, then we have usually managed to deliver effective training.

All of this may seem like an enormous amount of work. There is just no getting around the fact, I am afraid, that to deliver effective training does take a lot of hard work, but if you prepare yourself and your materials properly, it will all be worth it in the end. This is where the ADDIE model of instructional design can be a life-saver. If you follow the guidelines as suggested by the ADDIE model, in whatever sequence you prefer, the result will be a programme that leaves nothing to chance. The good news too, is that it also gets much easier every time you develop a programme.

On that positive note, I am going to follow my own advice and leave you with a thought-provoking quote from a colleague of mine:

> I have come to realise that in a classroom I can't possibly influence all my students. I am contented if I can touch just one life. That's good enough for me. (Ling Ai Li, Alice – lecturer, Singapore)

Appendix A
A survey of learning styles

Record the key letter next to the response that best describes your choice. You can choose more than one letter. Don't spend too much time thinking, as your first response is usually the one that best applies to your style of learning. If you really cannot decide, you may leave the question out.

1. You are about to give directions to a person. She is staying in a hotel in town and wants to visit your house. She has a rental car. Would you:

   V) Draw a map on paper?

   A) Tell her the directions?

   R) Write down the directions (without a map)?

   K) Collect her from the hotel in your car?

2. You are staying in a hotel and have a rental car. You would like to visit a friend whose address/location you do not know. Would you like them to:

   V) Draw you a map on paper?

   A) Tell you the directions?

   R) Write down the directions (without a map)?

   K) Collect you from the hotel in their car?

3. You have just received a copy of your schedule for a world trip. This is of interest to a friend. Would you:

    A) Call her immediately and tell her about it?

    R) Send her a copy of the printed schedule?

    V) Show her on a map of the world?

4. You are going to cook a dessert as a special treat for your family. Do you:

    K) Cook something familiar without need for instructions?

    V) Thumb through the cookbook looking for ideas from the pictures?

    R) Refer to a specific cookbook where there is a good recipe?

    A) Ask for advice from others?

5. A group of tourists has been assigned to you to find out about your home town. Would you:

    K) Drive them through it?

    V) Show them slides and photographs of it?

    R) Give them a book on it?

    A) Give them a talk on it?

6. You are about to purchase a new stereo. Other than price, what would most influence your decision?

    A) A friend talking about it?

    R) Reading the details about it?

    K) Listening to it?

    V) Its distinctive, upscale appearance?

7. Recall a time in your life when you learned how to do something like playing a new board game. Avoid

choosing a very physical skill like riding a bike. How did you learn best? By:

V) Visual clues – pictures, diagrams charts?

R) Written instructions?

A) Listening to somebody explaining it?

K) Doing it?

8. Which of these games do you prefer?

V) Pictionary?

R) Scrabble?

K) Charades?

9. You are about to learn to use a new program on a computer. Would you:

K) Ask a friend to show you?

R) Read the manual which comes with the program?

A) Telephone a friend and ask questions about it?

10. You are not sure whether a word should be spelled 'dependent' or 'dependant'. Do you:

R) Look it up in the dictionary?

A) Sound it out in your mind?

K) Write both versions down?

V) See the work in your mind and choose the best way it looks?

11. Apart from price, what would most influence your decisions to buy a particular textbook?

K) Using a friend's copy?

A) A friend talking about it?

R) Skimming parts of it?

V) It looks OK?

12. A new movie has arrived in town. What would most influence your decision to go or not go?

    A) Friends talked about it?

    R) You read a review about it?

    V) You saw a preview of it?

13. Do you prefer a lecturer/teacher who likes to use:

    R) Handouts and/or a textbook?

    K) Field trips, labs, practical sessions?

    V) Flow diagrams, charts, slides?

    A) Discussion, guest speakers?

End of survey

Scoring

Count the number of times you have recorded each key letter. The letter that appears the most number of times will give you an indication of your preferred style of learning. Remember that it is possible to have a mixed style of learning where no single key letter takes precedence over the others.

Note

This survey was published in *The Teaching Professor* (1993) Magna Publications (*http://www.magnapubs.com*): Madison, Wisconsin. Adapted here with permission from the publisher. The survey was found in Nurrenbern, S. C. (ed.) (1995) *Experiences in Cooperative Learning: A Collection for Chemistry Teachers*. Institute for Chemical Education, University of Wisconsin-Madison. Available at: *http://www.chem.purdue.edu/chm115/ Purdue_Customers/Learning_Style/learning_style.html* (last accessed: 13 April 2005).

Appendix B
Lesson plans

Lesson plan for beginners

Lesson title: Library Research Skills Workshop.

Course: Applied Science 1.

Audience: First-year polytechnic students, freshmen.

Venue: Library Training Room.

Duration: 90 minutes. (Note: this time would be for a class size of about 30. The lesson can take longer if the class size is larger, but you can cut down on the time needed by using facilitators to help keep the trainees on track).

Prerequisites: (a) ability to perform basic functions in the Windows operating system; (b) working knowledge of Internet Explorer or Netscape.

Description: This lesson is intended to introduce freshmen polytechnic students to the library's research resources.

Objectives: By the end of the training session the students will have learned to:

- Locate the links for OPAC and the research gateway (MetaLib) on the library website.

- Formulate a search strategy for use on any online database using keywords.
- Refine a search strategy using the Boolean operators AND, OR, NOT.
- Use OPAC to find the call numbers and locations of books related to the topics for their first assignments.
- Recognise in OPAC when a library book has been borrowed, and if it is out, when it is due to be returned.
- Select the library's research gateway (MetaLib) when looking for journal articles online.
- Locate full-text articles from the research gateway on the topic of their choice.
- Print, save or e-mail the results of a gateway search for their personal use.
- Evaluate the usefulness of websites according to the specified criteria as laid out in the website <give URL>.
- Use the APA citation style correctly when citing their references.

Materials: The following resources will be necessary:

- One computer with Internet access for each trainee (with a maximum number of two trainees per PC).
- One computer with Internet access for the trainer.
- Electronic classroom with video/data projector and overhead screen.

- PowerPoint presentation either on the desktop or loaded onto the library website.

- Presentation backup on at least two forms of electronic storage devices that are compatible with the trainer's PC.

- Online evaluation form plus backup hard copies of the form in case of access problems.

- Small gifts, if possible.

- Attention grabber resources, e.g. software that allows you to control all the computers in the training room, or music CD, and CD player preferably with batteries to eliminate the need to scramble for power cables and adapters and so on.

Handouts: Library pamphlets or guides on OPAC, MetaLib, advanced Web searching, and citing sources.

Content outline

Introduction	Resources
■ Hand out pamphlets/guides before the actual start of the lesson.	Pamphlets/guides.
■ Briefly introduce yourself when everyone has settled down.	PC remote control software in Library training room OR CD player and music CD in school labs.
■ Standing silently in front of the students usually quietens them down.	
■ Dive into the attention grabber.	
■ Provide the workshop synopsis.	(10 minutes)

OPAC	Resources
■ Provide the Library website URL.	PowerPoint presentation on Library website.
■ Show students where to find OPAC on Library website, then ask them to solve the first problem.	OPAC.
Problem 1: Does the Library have any books telling you how to raise guppies?	Model answer = guppies = 0, fish = 189.
■ Allow time for students to find answers. ■ Roam the floor and provide guidance if necessary. ■ When the students are done, explain how you would have conducted the search using keywords and other subjects as suggested by some of the results. ■ Explain all the options onscreen, e.g. phrase searching and title searching.	Browse detail screen of search results to find relevant subject links, e.g. aquariums. The point of the exercise is to highlight the fact that the first keywords used may not find any results. One needs to think of synonyms.
■ Explain how Booleans AND, OR, NOT help to refine a search.	(20 minutes)
MetaLib/research gateway	**Resources**
■ Explain the concept of articles and journals, i.e. the currency of their information as opposed to the information from books.	PowerPoint presentation on library website.
■ Show students how to access the research gateway and how to select the appropriate database set. ■ Demonstrate a search. ■ Set the problem.	Research gateway.
Problem 2: Find journal articles on 'genetically modified food' ■ Allow time for the students to find articles.	Search strategy: 'genetically modified' AND 'food'.

MetaLib/research gateway	Resources
■ Show the students how you would have conducted the search OR demonstrate a successful peer search – talk about narrowing a search by browsing the first set of results, and using a subject search.	(20 minutes)
World Wide Web	**Resources**
Problem 3: Can I trust the information on the following site? <provide URL of a dodgy site>. ■ Allow time for the students to find the answers as to why the site should not be trusted. ■ Use link to explain evaluating web sites <provide URL of a good website>.	PowerPoint presentation on library website. Dodgy website URL. (10 minutes)
Citing sources	**Resources**
■ Brief explanation of the importance of citing and plagiarism. ■ Provide links to reputable APA citation style websites.	Powerpoint presentation on Library website. APA citation style URLs (10 minutes)
The end	**Resources**
■ Wrap up with a revision of the objectives. ■ Survey.	Online survey. Small bribes (gifts or prizes) to encourage filling in of survey. (10 minutes)

Advanced lesson plan

Lesson title: Advanced Library Research Skills.

Course: Design 3.

Audience: Third-year polytechnic students.

Venue: Library Training Room.

Duration: 90 minutes (Note: this time would be for a class size of about 30. The lesson can take longer if the class size is larger, but you can cut down on the time needed by using facilitators to help keep the trainees on track).

Prerequisites: (a) ability to perform basic functions in the Windows operating system; (b) working knowledge of Internet Explorer or Netscape; (c) knowledge of basic searches using the library OPAC.

Description: This lesson is intended to show third-year polytechnic students how to make more efficient use of the library's research resources.

Objectives: By the end of the training session the students will have learned to:

- Limit a search by collection and/or type of material using the OPAC advanced search feature.

- Use the OPAC advanced search feature to locate journal titles held by the library in the design and fine arts subjects.

- Identify the bound journal issues held by the library.

- Identify which journal issues are allowed to be borrowed.

- Select the library research gateway (MetaLib) when searching for journal articles.

- Locate article citations from research gateway on topics with the design and fine arts areas.

- Identify the availability in OPAC of an article whose details were located using the research gateway.

- Refine a World Wide Web search by using phrase searching and Boolean operators.

- Evaluate information found on the Web according to the criteria specified during the workshop.

- Use the APA citation style correctly and consistently when citing references.

Materials: The following resources will be necessary:

- One computer with Internet access for each trainee (with a maximum number of two trainees per PC).

- One computer with Internet access for the trainer.

- Electronic classroom with video/data projector and overhead screen.

- PowerPoint presentation either on the desktop or loaded onto the library website.

- Presentation backup on some form of electronic storage device that is compatible with the trainer's PC.

- Online evaluation form plus backup hard copies of the form in case of access problems.

- Small gifts, if possible.

Handouts: Library pamphlets or guides on OPAC, MetaLib, advanced Web searching, and citing sources.

Content outline

Introduction	Resources
▪ Hand out pamphlets/guides before the actual start of the lesson.	Pamphlets/guides.
▪ Briefly introduce yourself and the workshop contents when everyone has settled down. Standing silently in front of the students usually quietens them down.	(10 minutes)

OPAC	Resources
Use the first problem as the attention grabber by asking the question before you do anything else. Don't even provide the Library website URL.	PowerPoint presentation.
Problem 1 – Find 3 journals in the library on the subject of ... something related to the design courses, e.g. product design.	OPAC.
▪ Allow roughly 10 minutes for students to find the answer.	
▪ Roam the floor and provide guidance if necessary.	
▪ When they have completed the task, demonstrate how you would use the OPAC advanced search feature to find journal titles in the library.	
▪ Make it clear that they can find the journal titles, but not the articles.	(15 minutes)

MetaLib/research gateway	Resources
Problem 2 – Find an online database devoted to the subject of ... something related to the design courses, e.g. architecture.	PowerPoint presentation.
▪ Allow approximately 10 minutes for the students to find an answer.	

MetaLib/research gateway	Resources
■ Roam the floor and provide guidance if necessary. ■ Once the first student has provided an answer, demonstrate a MetaLib search for a list of online databases, explaining the various options available to them. ■ Emphasise the currency of journal articles as opposed to the information found in books. *Problem 3 – Find a journal article on the subject of … something related to design, e.g. lightwave.* ■ Again, allow time for them to search and roam the floor to provide guidance. ■ When the students have completed the task, demonstrate a MetaLib search for journal articles. ■ Explain the various options provided.	Research gateway. (20 minutes)
World Wide Web	**Resources**
Problem 4 – Find a website that explains Boolean operators. ■ Allow time for students to find the answer and read the explanation. ■ Roam the floor to provide guidance. ■ Demonstrate a Google search showing the different results using phrase searches and adding more keywords. ■ Explain and demonstrate that these search strategies can be used on OPAC, MetaLib too, pointing out Boolean selection options.	PowerPoint presentation. keywords: web design (by itself) 'web design' (as a phrase) 'web design' bad (add a word) (10 minutes)

Evaluating sources	Resources
■ Reinforce the importance of evaluating the information they find during their research. ■ Provide various reputable website URLs on this topic.	PowerPoint presentation. (5 minutes)
Citing sources	**Resources**
■ Reinforce the importance of citing and plagiarism. ■ Provide links to reputable APA citation style websites.	PowerPoint presentation on Library website. (5 minutes)
The end	**Resources**
■ Wrap up with a brief recap of the objectives. ■ Online survey.	Online survey. Small bribes (gifts or prizes) to encourage filling in of survey. (10 minutes)

Lesson plan for online tutorial

Lesson title: Spark Online Skills.

Audience: First-year polytechnic students, freshmen.

Venue: Via Blackboard or WebCT learning systems.

Duration: Four hours. (This is an estimate, some students may take longer, and others will complete it in much less than four hours). The tutorial is made available to the students for the period of one semester.

Prerequisites: (a) ability to perform basic functions in the Windows operating system; (b) working knowledge of Internet Explorer or Netscape; (c) working knowledge of Blackboard or

WebCT; (d) network access (i.e. functioning user name and password).

Description: This lesson is intended to introduce freshmen polytechnic students to the library's research resources. It is offered online so the students can complete it in their own time.

Objectives: By the end of the training session the students will have learned to:

- Identify general sources of information that will help increase familiarity with a topic.
- Define or modify the information need to achieve a manageable focus.
- Identify key concepts and terms that describe the information need.
- Identify the differences between potential resources in a variety of formats.
- Differentiate between primary and secondary sources.
- Identify keywords, synonyms, and related terms for the information need.
- Identify search language and protocols (e.g. truncation).
- Identify the scope and content of the various library information retrieval (IR) systems.
- Use various search systems to retrieve information in a variety of formats.
- Implement a search strategy using appropriate commands for the IR system selected (e.g. Booleans).

- Use the Library of Congress classification scheme to identify the location of information resources within the library.

- Retrieve a document in electronic format.

- Assess the quantity, quality, and relevance of the search results to determine whether alternate IR systems should be used.

- Examine information from various sources in order to evaluate reliability, relevancy, completeness, authority, and currency.

- Identify the elements and correct syntax of a citation for a wide range of sources.

- Select the appropriate documentation style and use it consistently to cite sources.

Materials: The following resources will be necessary for the *students*:

- A computer with Internet access.

- Browser – at least Netscape 3.0 or Explorer 4.0.

- Adobe Acrobat Reader software for PDF files.

- Flash plug-in.

The following resources will be necessary for the *course designer*:

- Dreamweaver, Frontpage, or knowledge of HTML coding.

- Flash.

- Fireworks, Photoshop, or other graphics editing software.

- Blackboard Learning System.

Handouts: None.

Content outline

Introduction	Resources
■ Brief introduction to the online tutorial. ■ Link to the content page.	■ Web page accessed via Blackboard. ■ Content page to open in a new window, outside of Blackboard, to provide more screen space.
Module 1 – Starting Your Research	**Resources**
Overview (big picture) of the module. Contents... ■ Defining and understanding an assignment topic. ■ Identifying keywords and concepts. ■ Identifying different sources of information. ■ Developing a search strategy. ■ Review of the objectives.	■ *http://lii.org/* ■ Mind map examples. ■ Interactive quizzes (Flash) to reinforce learning. ■ Animated demonstrations of the three Boolean operators AND, OR, NOT
Module 2 – Searching for Information	**Resources**
Overview of the module. Contents... ■ What material is held by the library. ■ OPAC explained. ■ How to access OPAC. ■ Animated demonstration of searching OPAC. ■ The difference between books and journal articles, e.g. currency, how to search for them. ■ MetaLib explained. ■ Searching MetaLib step-by-step in pictures.	■ OPAC basic search demonstration (Flash). ■ Guided hands-on OPAC search (create a web page that frames OPAC, so you have a frame section to include guidance instructions). ■ Interactive quiz on OPAC. ■ Access to MetaLib for hands-on exercise. ■ Interactive quiz on MetaLib.

Module 2 – Searching for Information	Resources
■ LexisNexis Academic (LNA) explained, i.e. access to newspapers online. ■ Accessing LNA. ■ Searching LNA step-by-step in pictures. ■ Discussion of common myths about the World Wide Web, e.g. everything can be found on the Web, everything is free. ■ Benefits of advanced Web searching using Google and Yahoo. ■ How to access and use the advanced search features in Google and Yahoo. ■ Review of the module objectives	■ Guided hands-on LNA search (don't forget to get permission from LNA to frame their site with your instructions). ■ Interactive quiz on LNA. ■ URLs of dodgy websites. ■ *http://www.google.com* ■ *http://www.yahoo.com* ■ PDF file on Internet domains, including a list of country domains. ■ PDF explained, including a link to download the Adobe Reader software. ■ Interactive quiz.
Module 3 – Evaluating and citing	**Resources**

Overview of the module.
Contents…
■ Why evaluation of resources is necessary.
■ How to evaluate according to the following criteria:
  – authority
  – completeness
  – currency
  – reliability
  – relevancy.
■ Why citing of the information is necessary.
■ When to cite the sources.
■ American Psychological Association citation style explained.
	■ Interactive quiz.
	
	■ URLs of reputable websites showing how to cite according to APA style.
	■ Interactive quizzes to give students practice at recognising the different parts of citations.

Module 3 – Evaluating and citing	Resources
■ Parts of a citation for books, newspapers and web pages explained. ■ Review of the objectives.	■ PDF file giving examples of citing other sources of information. ■ Interactive quiz.
Final test or quiz	**Resources**
■ A final test or quiz to see how many of the learning objectives have been met. ■ You can show the students the results immediately, or send the marks to the lecturer. ■ You can also include an optional opinion survey, but don't expect all the students to complete it.	■ Multiple choice quiz (easier for the trainer to mark). ■ Opinion survey

Appendix C
Select annotated bibliography of the instructional experiences of other librarians

- Asner, H. and Polani, T. (2004) 'Building a required, virtual, voice-supported library skills course: an Israeli experience', *Reference Services Review* 32(3): 256–63.

Librarians from the Aranne Central Library of the Ben-Gurion University, Israel, describe their use of a web-based learning content management system to develop an online tutorial. Consisting of PowerPoint slides with animation and voice-over, the two short lessons of this tutorial provide a general introduction to the library for first-year students, with the emphasis being on searching OPAC. Interesting to note are the lessons learned from the recording of the voice-overs.

- Bodi, S. (2002) 'How do we bridge the gap between what we teach and what they do? Some thoughts on the place of questions in the process of research'. *Journal of Academic Librarianship* 28(3): 109–14.

Bodi highlights the difference between the research methods of scholars and undergraduates, identifying three main problem areas as experienced by the students. Namely, how to select a suitable topic, how to conduct subject searches, and how to evaluate the information found. The biggest hurdle faced by the students is that they have to begin their research knowing nothing about their topic. The author also provides some very useful questions that you can get your trainees to ask themselves in order to decide upon, and bring focus to their topic.

- Castro, G. M. (2002) 'From workbook to Web: building an information literacy oasis', *Computers in Libraries* 22(1): 30–5.

Castro describes the development of the Online Advancement of Student Information Skills (OASIS) tutorial by the San Francisco State University. An existing self-paced programme, along with a set of 11 core competencies formed the foundation of this online tutorial. Notable is the approach taken with the assessment questions, that is, random generation from a pool of questions. The author has also provided a very useful link to some sample quiz questions.

- Cullen, R. (2005) 'Empowering patients through health information literacy training', *Health Education* 54(4): 231–44.

This article stresses the importance of information literacy skills in a time when all kinds of medical information is freely available on the Internet. In order to be able to make informed decisions and look after the health of themselves and their families, it is vital that people know how to evaluate the information they find. Five principles of good teaching and learning are provided, along with an extremely useful list of learning objectives.

- Dewald, N. H. (1999) 'Transporting good library instruction practices into the Web environment: an analysis of online tutorials', *Journal of Academic Librarianship* 25(1): 26–31.

Dewald discusses seven features of good library instruction as applied to the online situation, with examples of how these features were incorporated into some 20 online programmes. The difficulties of trying to include all of these features into an online tutorial are described, with the conclusion being that online programmes cannot stand alone but need to be used in conjunction with some form of face-to-face training.

■ Enger, K. B., Brenenson, S., Lenn, K., MacMillan, M., Meisart, M. F., Meserve, H. and Vella, S. A. (2002) 'Problem-based learning: evolving strategies and conversations for library instruction', *Reference Services Review* 30(4): 355–8.

The findings from a LOEX-of-the-West pre-conference workshop, this article provides a simple explanation of what problem-based learning actually is, as well as a list of guidelines that you can use when designing a short library training session. For anyone wanting to include problem-based learning in their training, the template presented here would be very useful.

■ Frantz, P. (2002) 'A scenario-based approach to credit course instruction', *Reference Services Review* 30(1): 37–42.

Frantz proposes that we use the questions asked at the library reference counter as the basis for information literacy instruction. The pros and cons of such an approach are discussed, along with ten scenario examples. The link for the course content is no longer active, but quite a bit of detail is provided for each scenario.

■ McMillen, P. S., Miyagishima, B. and Maughan, L. S. (2002) 'Lessons learned about developing and coordinating an instruction program with freshman composition', *Reference Services Review* 30(4): 288–99.

This article looks at the development of an instruction programme for first-year students by the Oregon State

University Libraries in 2001. Included are the valuable lessons that were learned about what is needed to start and maintain such a programme, with particular emphasis on the competencies needed by the librarians involved.

- Noe, N. W. and Bishop, B. A. (2005) 'Assessing Auburn University Library's Tiger Information Literacy Tutorial (TILT)', *Reference Services Review* 33(2): 173–87.

Noe and Bishop discuss the effectiveness of their Tiger Information Literacy Tutorial which was adapted from the Texas Information Literacy Tutorial (TILT). Overall the tutorial was found to be effective as indicated by the pre- and post-tests. You will find these tests and a student perception survey in the appendices of this article.

- Phillips, L. and Kearley, J. (2003) 'TIP: tutorial for information power and campus-wide information literacy', *Reference Services Review* 31(4): 351–8.

Discussed here is the impact of the Tutorial for Information Power (TIP) programme at the University of Wyoming Libraries. This article points to TIP as being partly instrumental in getting information literacy an embedded course requirement on campus.

- Rutter, L. and Matthews, M. (2002) 'Infoskills: a holistic approach to on-line user education', *The Electronic Library* 20(1): 29–34.

Looks at the development of a web-based library tutorial at Bournemouth University in the UK. The librarians list their key objectives, and provide a very useful set of key functions that include the use of active learning and having a consistent look and feel to the web pages. The URL for the tutorial is also given.

Bibliography

Allan, B. (2003) *Training Skills for Library Staff.* Lanham, MD: Scarecrow Press.

Association of College and Research Libraries (2005) *Objectives for Information Literacy Instruction: A Model for Academic Librarians.* Available from: *http://www.ala.org/ala/acrl/acrlstandards/objectivesinformation.htm* (last accessed: 15 August 2005).

Barkley, S. and Bianco, T. (2001) 'Learning experts examine shortfalls in on-site and on-line training', *Supervision* 62(1): 11–13.

Brandt, D. S. (2002) *Teaching Technology: A How-To-Do-It Manual for Librarians.* New York, NY: Neal-Schuman Publishers.

Chambers and Associates (1997) *Chunking Principle.* Available from: *http://www.chambers.com.au/glossary/chunk.htm* (last accessed: 16 February 2005).

Clark, D. (1995) *Introduction to Instructional System Design.* Available from: *http://www.nwlink.com/~donclark/hrd/sat1.html* (last accessed: 14 March 2005).

Delahoussaye, M. (2002) 'The perfect learner: an expert debate on learning styles', *Training* 39(5): 28–36.

Dowling, N. L. and McKinnon, S. H. (2002) 'Instructional objectives: improving the success of safety training', *Professional Safety*, September: 41–4.

Fowler, C. S. and Dupuis, E. A. (2000) 'What have we done? TILT's impact on our instruction program', *Reference Services Review* 28(4): 343–8.

Grammatis, Y. (1998) *Learning Styles*. Available from: *http://www.chaminade.org/inspire/learnstl.htm* (last accessed: 14 April 2005).

Hiemstra, R. and Sisco, B. (1990) *Individualizing Instruction*. San Francisco, CA: Jossey-Bass.

Instructional Technology Services, Texas A&M University (2001) *ADDIE: Instructional Design Model*. Available from: *http://itsinfo.tamu.edu/workshops/handouts/pdf_handouts/addie.pdf* (last accessed: 5 May 2004).

Jolles, R. L. (2001) *How to Run Seminars and Workshops: Presentation Skills for Consultants, Trainers, and Teachers*. 2nd edn. New York: John Wiley and Sons.

Krathwohl, D. R. (2002) 'A revision of Bloom's taxonomy: an overview', *Theory into Practice* 41(4): 212–18.

Lindauer, B. G. (2004) 'The three arenas of information literacy assessment', *Reference and User Services Quarterly* 44(2): 122–9.

Macklin, A. S. (2001) 'Integrating information literacy using problem-based learning', *Reference Services Review* 29(4): 306–14.

Middleton, A. (2005) 'An attempt to quantify the quality of student bibliographies', *International Journal for Library and Information Services* 6(1): 7–18.

Molberg, A. (2003) *Making Live Training Lively! 50 Tips for Engaging your Audience*. Boston, MA: Course Technology.

Molenda, M. (2003) *In Search of the Elusive ADDIE Model*. Available from: *http://www.indiana.edu/~molpage/In Search of Elusive ADDIE* (last accessed: 4 April 2005).

Nielsen, J. (2005) *Top Ten Web Design Mistakes of 2005*. Available from: *http://www.useit.com/alertbox/designmistakes.html* (last accessed: 31 October 2005).

Open Learning Technology Corporation (1996) *Conditions of Learning*. Available from: *http://www.educationau.edu.au/archives/cp/04d.htm* (last accessed: 18 April 2005).

Ondrusek, A., Dent, Valeda F., Bonadie-Joseph, I. & Williams, C. (2005) 'A longitudinal study of the development and evaluation of an information literacy test', *Reference Services Review* 33(4): 388–417.

Phillips, L. and Kearley, J. (2003) 'TIP: tutorial for information power and campus-wide information literacy'. *Reference Services Review* 31(4): 351–8.

Sherman, R. (2002) '10 presentation skills top executives live by'. *Business Credit* (June): 46–7.

Small, R. V. (1997) *Motivation in Instructional Design. Eric Digest*. Available from: *http://www.ericdigests.org/1998-1/motivation.htm* (last accessed: 19 April 2005).

Smith, M. K. (1999) *Andragogy, the Encyclopaedia of Informal Education*. Available from: *http://www.infed.org/lifelonglearning/b-andra.htm* (last accessed: 19 April 2005).

Stolovitch, H. D. and Keeps, E. J. (2003) *Telling Ain't Training*. Alexandria, VA: ASTD.

Tittel, E. (2004) 'Learning with style: what's your learning personality?' *Certification Magazine* 6(11): 16–21.

Visscher-Voerman, I. and Gustafson, K. L. (2004) 'Paradigms in the theory and practice of education and training design', *Educational Technology Research and Development* 52(2): 69–89.

Wallace, M. (2001) *Twelve Sure Fire Ways to Torpedo Your Presentations*. Available from: *http://www.llrx.com/columns/guides54.htm* (last accessed: 28 September 2004).

Watson, S. (2002) 'A lesson in training', *Security Management* 46(10): 75–81.

Workshops by Thiagi, Inc (2003) *Laws of Learning*. Available from: *http://www.thiagi.com/laws-of-learning .html* (last accessed: 15 August 2005).

Wilder, C. and Rotondo, J. (2002) *Point, Click and Wow! A Quick Guide to Brilliant Laptop Presentations.* San Francisco, CA: Jossey-Bass/Pfeiffer.

Williams, J. L. (2000) 'Creativity in assessment of library instruction', *Reference Services Review* 28(4): 323–35.

Zemke, R. (2002) 'A pocket guide to useful learning theories'. *Training* 39(9): 90–1.

Index